Regional Sea Kayaking Series

Guide to Sea Kayaking on Lakes Huron, Erie & Ontario

The Best Day Trips and Tours

by

Sarah Ohmann and Bill Newman

The Globe Pequot Press

Guilford, Connecticut

Cover design: Adam Schwartzman
Text design: Casey Shain
Cover photograph: © Gary Nelkie/Nordic Sports, East Tawas, Michigan
Maps by: Mary Ballachino
Interior photos by: Bill Newman and Sarah Ohmann

Library of Congress Cataloging-in-Publication Data

Newman, William.
    Guide to sea kayaking on lakes Huron, Erie & Ontario: the best day trips and tours/by William Newman and Sarah Ohmann. — 1st ed.
        p.   cm. (Regional sea kayaking series)
    Includes index.
    ISBN 0-7627-0417-9
    1. Sea kayaking—Huron, Lake (Mich. and Ont.) Guidebooks.
2. Sea kayaking—Erie, Lake Guidebooks. 3. Sea kayaking—Ontario, Lake (N.Y. and Ont.) Guidebooks. 4. Huron, Lake (Mich. and Ont.) Guidebooks. 5. Erie, Lake Guidebooks. 6. Ontario, Lake (N.Y. and Ont.) Guidebooks. I. Ohmann, Sarah. II. Title. III. Series
GV776.H87N49   1999
917.404'33—DC21   99-25249
                                                                              CIP

Manufactured in the United States of America
First Edition/First Printing

Contents

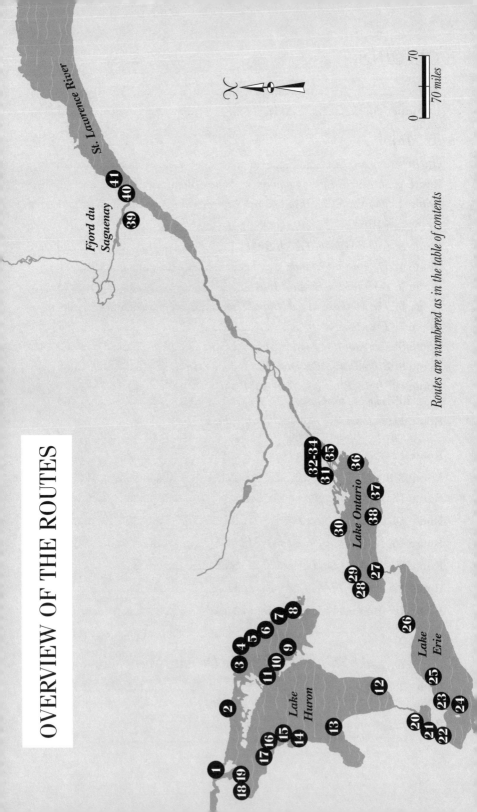

OVERVIEW OF THE ROUTES

St. Lawrence River

Fjord du Saguenay

Lake Ontario

Lake Erie

Lake Huron

Routes are numbered as in the table of contents

70 miles

Preface

When I first moved from Seattle to the Midwest in 1990, I felt very glum indeed about the prospect of being landlocked in such a flat and featureless place. I missed the mountains and the ocean badly and dreamed of going back west after finishing school. Even the Boundary Waters, I felt, didn't measure up to the landscape of the Pacific Northwest or the hills of New England where I grew up. One day on my way back from a canoeing trip in the Arrowhead of Minnesota, I took the shoreline road instead of the inland route and ended by standing, amazed, on the north shore of Lake Superior as the waves rolled in. I had no idea that such a wildly beautiful place existed in the middle of the continent, or that the Great Lakes were capable of such weather and waves. Within two months I had a kayak and was tentatively venturing out on the water. Within a few years I found that I no longer wanted to move west again, that the western landscape no longer measured up to the country I found here. I hope this book will help you find your way to some of the last, best places, anywhere.

—*Sarah Ohmann*

I bought my first sea kayak a little over ten years ago, while living on the shores of West Grand Traverse Bay on the Old Mission Peninsula. Having paddled white water for years, I was a bit worried that sea kayaking would be dull. Confident in my skills from paddling white water, I was surprised to feel uncomfortable being as little as a mile offshore. Three years later, I found myself in the middle of Lake Michigan, 40 miles from the nearest shore. Our group of four paddled almost thirty hours to cross 80 miles of open water. Paddling all day, all night, and on into the next day gives you a unique perspective on the size of these freshwater seas. Paddling in stormy November seas at the Gales of November Rendezvous in Agawa Bay removed all doubts about sea kayaking being dull and gave me an appreciation for the awesome power of the lakes. Kayaking the Great Lakes is not just for thrill junkies. Without a sea kayak I would never have entered beautifully sculpted sea caves, played hide-and-seek with a family otters, shared a cobblestone beach with a timber wolf, or watched an incredible display of northern lights far from the pollution of city lights. I hope this book will help you explore the lakes and find your own adventures.

—*Bill Newman*

Introduction

Those who haven't explored the Great Lakes may be surprised to find that they have some of the best sea kayaking in the country: sand beaches, tall cliffs, long stretches of undeveloped shoreline with excellent wilderness camping, beautiful rock formations, sand dunes hundreds of feet high, and some very fine sea caves. The Eastern Great Lakes have an incredible variety of shoreline: thousands of islands made of smooth ancient rock in Georgian Bay, the towering dolomite cliffs of the Niagara Escarpment on the Bruce Peninsula, and the narrow sand beaches, shoals, and marshes of northern Lake Erie. Although much of the shoreline of the Eastern Great Lakes has been developed, northern Lake Huron and Georgian Bay still have many miles of wilderness shoreline and thousands of wilderness islands to explore. Farther south, even near the large population centers on Lake Erie and Lake Ontario, there are many parks that contain protected islands and shoreline.

At the edge of the Canadian Shield, the islands and rocky shores of Georgian Bay and the Thousand Islands have some of the oldest rock formations on the planet, some almost four billion years old. The spectacular white dolomite cliffs of the Niagara Escarpment run along the eastern side of the Bruce Peninsula and out into the islands at the mouth of Georgian Bay. The Niagara Escarpment marks the edge of an ancient sea that once extended from Rochester, New York, across Ontario to Michigan. Sections of southern Lake Huron, Lake Saint Clair, and Lake Erie have low sand beaches or small coastal sand dunes. On Lake Saint Clair and Lake Erie, the shoals and large flats have created large marshes, which provide rich feeding areas for millions of migratory birds. The forests of the Eastern Great Lakes are a mixture of conifers and deciduous trees, such as eastern white pine, eastern hemlock, yellow birch, red pine, sugar maple, red oak, and basswood, with the deciduous trees more common to the southern lakes. Along the northern shore of Lake Erie are remnants of Carolinian forest, which includes many plants normally associated with the southern United States, including sassafras and tulip trees. The Carolinian forest also supports many species of animals that are not normally found as far north in the Great Lakes.

The Eastern Great Lakes also have a rich maritime history. As early as 1783 work had begun on canals along the St. Lawrence River, and by 1900 a complete network of canals and waterways allowed shallow-draft vessels to travel from Lake Superior to the St. Lawrence River as far as Montreal. With the opening of the Welland Canal in 1959, there was at last a deepwater connection along the St. Lawrence Seaway, allowing freight from any of the Great Lakes to travel all the way to the Atlantic Ocean. Today about forty million tons of cargo pass through the St. Lawrence River between the Atlantic and the Great Lakes each year. The Great Lakes have a dark history as well, which includes thousands of vessels that never returned to port. On the Eastern Lakes there are several areas that were notorious for shipwrecks near the turn of the century. At the tip of the Bruce Peninsula within the Fathom Five Park are over twenty historical shipwrecks. Lake Huron's Thunder Bay Region was often called the "shipwreck coast," with more than 160 known shipwrecks. The Pelee Passage between Point Pelee and Pelee Island is known to have sent more than 275 ships to the bottom of Lake Erie.

Sea Kayak Safety

The power of the Great Lakes should not be taken lightly. Although they are called lakes, don't mistake them for millponds. The day after finishing the last trip for this guidebook, we heard that the first November gale of the season brought 80-knot winds and 20-foot waves to Lake Superior. The lakes have wrecked thousands of ships and claimed the lives of kayakers as well. Make sure you're prepared before paddling the routes described in this book.

Equipment

Don't leave shore without a seaworthy kayak with watertight bulkheads and/or flotation bags, a personal flotation device (PFD), bilge pump, compass, and paddle float. Just as important as having this safety equipment is knowing how to use it. Those who are getting started in the sport should take classes, join a club, or learn from more experienced paddlers. Regardless of their experience level, all kayakers should practice self-rescue and assisted-rescue techniques until they are automatic. Most important of all is your good judgment, which can save you from having to use rescue techniques and gadgets in the first place.

Trip Ratings

The trips in this book are rated by us as *beginner, intermediate,* or *advanced,* with the assumption that a beginning paddler (as opposed to a novice) will have a basic working knowledge of the common paddle strokes and braces, a paddle float self-rescue and at least one of the assisted rescues (such as the T rescue). Intermediate paddlers should be comfortable paddling in higher winds over 15 knots in waves of 2–4 feet and have the endurance to paddle 20 miles or more per day in good weather. They should be proficient in several group-rescue and self-rescue techniques, paddle-bracing skills, and learning the Eskimo roll.

Advanced paddlers should be able to paddle in very rough conditions, have strong bracing skills, and a reliable Eskimo roll—preferably on both sides. They should be comfortable paddling in winds up to 30 knots and be able to paddle 30 miles per day or more in good weather. Advanced paddlers should have mastered several group-rescue and self-rescue skills and be able to complete most rescues in less than one minute. In some cases advanced trips can be done with intermediate-level skills if extra time is allowed to wait out bad weather. Trip ratings are based on the assumption of paddling in good weather during the summer months. However the stormy weather of fall and spring—or sudden squalls at any time—can easily turn a trip rated at a beginner level into an advanced-level trip.

Weather

One of the recurring factors in deaths or near deaths on the Great Lakes seems to be a failure to check or to heed marine forecasts before setting out. Sudden squalls or changes in weather can cause rapid changes in wind and wave conditions, turning calm sunny days into a kayaker's worst nightmare. Be especially wary of the weather when making open-water crossings. Although many kayakers have completed these trips safely, we would like to emphasize that the longer the crossing, the greater the risk and chance of encountering a change in the weather or experiencing some other mishap. In many cases ferries or charter boats can be used to shuttle boats and gear to an island or start of a trip, and if you have limited experience with open-water paddling, please consider this as an option.

Another factor that must be considered is water temperature. Early in the season, particularly in the northern lakes, the surface temperature may be only a few degrees above freezing. Paddling on water this cold introduces an extra level of risk. Dress for the water temperature, not the air temperature: We strongly encourage the use of a wet suit or dry suit for cold-water paddling.

Maps

The maps that illustrate each trip give a general idea of the location of the places mentioned in the route descriptions and are not to be used for navigation: Refer to the nautical charts or topographic maps recom-mended for a route. All distances are given in statute miles as this is the usual custom for inland waters on U.S. charts (apologies to Canadian paddlers who will have to convert to kilometers). Global positioning system (GPS) waypoints are given for some of the landmarks mentioned in the trip descriptions, but do *not* rely on these as your sole means of navigation. We generated most waypoints using handheld GPS units (without DGPS correction) and have made a reasonable effort to ensure that these are correct, but you should check them against a nautical chart before using them, *especially* when making an open-water crossing. Even if you carry a GPS, make sure you carry a chart and compass and know how to navigate using them.

It is not our intention to scare people away from the sport. In nearly all cases sea kayaking accidents have involved boaters who did not learn basic skills or did not follow the basic safety rules that we have listed. The authors and our many kayaking friends have paddled thousands of miles without ever having a serious accident of any kind.

Whether you have a love of history, wildlife, or simply enjoy paddling along a beautiful coast, the Eastern Great Lakes have something to offer every paddler. We hope this book will help you explore all that the Eastern Lakes have to offer.

Lake Huron
Ontario

Route 1:

━━ ━━ ━━ ━━ ━━ ━━ ━━ ━━ ━━ ━━ ━━ ━━ ━━ ➤

St. Mary's River: Campement d'Ours Island

This trip circumnavigates one of the islands in the area where the St. Mary's River flows into the North Channel, a body of water partially separated from Lake Huron by the chain of islands ending with Manitoulin Island. The islands seen on this trip have steep granite bluffs covered with pines and other evergreens, making for a very pretty day paddle. Because the islands provide so much shelter, this is a good early or late season trip.

TRIP HIGHLIGHTS: Good scenery.

TRIP RATING:

Beginner: 4-mile trip from Kensington Point to Wilson Island and back; 7-mile trip from Gawas Bay to Wilson Island and back.
Intermediate: 9-mile loop around Campement d'Ours Island, starting at any of the launch sites.

TRIP DURATION: Part to full day.

NAVIGATION AIDS: Canadian Hydrographic Service (CHS) chart 14883, Canadian topographic map 41 J/5 at 1:50,000.

CAUTIONS: Boat traffic, some exposure to east winds.

TRIP PLANNING: This area is well known to boaters, so you can expect boat traffic—and it would be wise to avoid the summer holiday weekends. This route will be quieter before Victoria Day (first Monday preceding May 25), after Labor Day, or on week-nights. The Friends of the St. Mary's River have published a pamphlet with a map and guide to all of the St. Mary's River for paddlers. Call the Friends of the St. Mary's River at (705) 759–6191 to get a copy.

LAUNCH SITES: There are three possible launch sites for the loop:

Gawas Bay: There is a government boat launch at Gawas Bay with a small turnaround/parking lot. There are no facilities and no fees for parking or launching. On the other hand the lot will hold only a few cars, and on a busy day, you may have to try one of the other launches. From the intersection of Highways 17 and 548, go south on 548 to St. Joseph Island. Stay on Highway 548 through mile 3.3, where it makes a ninety-degree turn to the east. Continue on 548 until mile 5.8, then turn left onto Canoe Point Road. Drive another 0.2 mile to the bottom of the hill and the boat launch.

Highway 548 rest area: This spot has ample day-use parking, toilets, and is right on the water. The only disadvantage here is the current: Paddlers who launch from here should be certain that they can beat the current back upstream or set up a shuttle (at Gawas Bay, for example). Although the river was pretty quiet when we visited the site, other kayakers have told us that at high water there may be standing waves in the narrow channel between the mainland and St. Joseph Island. From the intersection of Highways 17 and 548, drive 1.6 miles south on 548 to a rest area on the west side of the road, just before the bridge.

Kensington Point: There is a marina here, and parking and launching fees may apply. Facilities are minimal, but this is the launch closest to the group of small islands west of Campement d'Ours (pronounced and even spelled locally as *Campador*) Island. From the town center of Desbarats on Highway 17 (next to the only gas station), drive 0.9 mile west on 17. Turn left/south onto Kensington Road and follow it for another 1.3 miles, where it comes to an end at Holder Marine.

DIRECTIONS

START: Start at the **Highway 548 rest area** and paddle southeast past the highway bridge and to the north side of **St. Joseph Island**.

MILE 1.5: Pass **Colter Island**. *Caution:* There is a line of shoals extending northwest from the tip of Colter Island toward Devils Island, some just under the surface. Continue paddling into **Bamagaseck Bay**.

MILE 2.5: The bay narrows to a tiny channel between St. Joseph and Campement d'Ours Islands. A small bridge connects the two islands, with about 4 feet of clearance above the water. Paddle on past several small islands, bays, and inlets. Please note that all the land is private here, so wait until the Gawas Bay boat launch to stretch your legs.

MILE 3.0: The narrow channel opens out into **Gawas Bay**. For those starting or stopping at the boat launch here, it is located on the southeast part of the bay; look for a small dock and the brown and white sign indicating a government launch.

MILE 3.5: Turn and follow the shore of Campement d'Ours Island to the northeast.

MILE 4.0: As you approach the eastern tip of the island, you will paddle by a string of small islands and rocks stretching toward **Portlock Island**. *Caution:* Gawas Bay opens out into the **St. Joseph Channel**, which looks

St. Mary's River: Campement d'Ours Island

ST. MARY'S RIVER:
Campement d'Ours Island

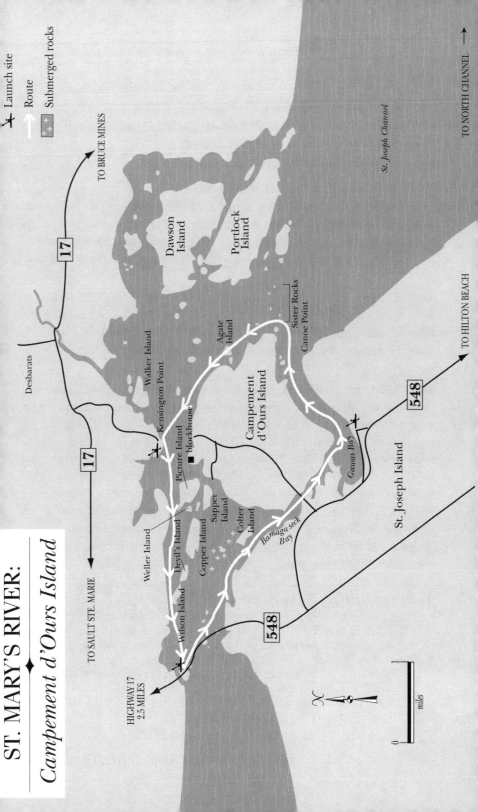

Launch site
Route
Submerged rocks

TO BRUCE MINES

17

TO NORTH CHANNEL →

St. Joseph Channel

Dawson Island

Portlock Island

Desbarats

17

Walker Island

Kensington Point

Agate Island

Sister Rocks
Canoe Point

Picture Island
■ blockhouse

Campement
d'Ours Island

TO HILTON BEACH

548

Gawas Bay

TO SAULT STE. MARIE

Weller Island

Devil's Island

Sapper Island

Copper Island

Colter Island

Bamagaseck Bay

St. Joseph Island

Wilson Island

548

HIGHWAY 17
2.5 MILES

miles
0   1

east toward the North Channel. Between **Canoe Point** and the **Sister Rocks**, you will be exposed to wind and waves from the southeast and east. Keep an eye out for shoals as you pass the Sister Rocks.

MILE 4.5: Round the eastern tip of Campement d'Ours Island and paddle to the northwest. *Sidetrip:* Add a trip to visit Dawson Island and Portlock Island, crossing St. Joseph Channel.

MILE 5.0: Pass by **Agate Island**, then follow the shore as it curves westward.

MILE 5.5: **Kensington Point** is to the north, the starting point for those paddling out to the small island group west of Campement d'Ours. As you pass the northernmost tip of Campement d'Ours, look for a **blockhouse** or fort tower on the point. This is not a fur trade original, but a replica built by one of the island's early owners who wanted to attract tourists to the area.

MILE 6.0: Pass **Picture Island**, the first in the island chain. Take some time to explore the islands and channel between Picture and **Sapper Islands**. There are few cottages in this attractive little island cluster, possibly because the steep rock walls have made building difficult. Continue paddling west.

MILE 7.5: The channel formed by the mainland and the island chain comes to an end at a small outlet at the tip of **Wilson Island**. There may be some current at the entrance here, and if it's too strong, beginning paddlers can exit through the gap between Wilson and Devils easily, and then return to Kensington Point via the southern side of the island chain. Paddlers who are returning to the Highway 548 rest area will have to fight their way upstream, although the current along the northern shore is not too bad. Paddlers who started at Gawas Bay should probably paddle directly south from Wilson to the north shore of St. Joseph Island, skipping the heaviest current near the highway bridge. (See Start to mile 3.0 for directions to complete the loop to the Gawas Bay boat launch.)

Where to Eat & Where to Stay

RESTAURANTS & LODGING The nearest facilities will be on St. Joseph Island, in towns such as Hilton Beach or Richard's Landing. Call the St. Joseph Island Chamber of Commerce at (705) 246–2581 for a map and a list of island businesses. **CAMPING** Try **Fred's Tent and Trailer Park** in Richard's Landing (705–246–2572) or **Hilton Beach Tourist Resort** (705–246–0063), both located on St. Joseph Island.

Route 2:
■ ■ ■ ■ ■ ■ ■ ■ ■ ■ ■ ■ ■ ■ ■ ➡

The North Channel: Spanish River to Aird Island

The North Channel is partially divided from the rest of Lake Huron by the islands of the northern rim of the Niagara Escarpment, including Drummond and Manitoulin Islands, which are made primarily of dolomite. On the north side of the channel, however, the geology is that of the Canadian Shield, and the weathered granite also seen on the east side of Lake Superior predominates. Between Serpent River and the Bay of Islands on the north side of Manitoulin are many small island groups. Although the area around Killarney has many cottages, the Whalesback Channel is still relatively undeveloped and a great place to explore by kayak. The islands near the mouth of the Spanish River (including Green Island) are composed of steep granite, and the pretty scenery makes the islands a good destination for a day paddle and a good introduction to the North Channel. A trip around Aird Island is also good day trip for those who want a longer paddle.

TRIP HIGHLIGHTS: Good scenery.

TRIP RATING:
Beginner: 7-mile trip around Green Island and back from the Spanish marina.
Intermediate: 20-mile trip around Aird Island and back.

TRIP DURATION: Full day.

NAVIGATION AIDS: CHG chart 2299, Canadian topographic map: *Spanish* (41 J/1) at 1:50,000.

CAUTIONS: Some boat traffic near the marina and in channels; some exposure to westerly and southerly winds on the south side of Aird Island.

TRIP PLANNING: Except for the south side of Aird Island, this route is very sheltered, and it is unlikely that you'll encounter more than a little chop in the Whalesback Channel, making this a good early or late season trip. The marina at Spanish expanded quite a bit in 1998, and this will probably mean a little more boat traffic in the area, but there are still many shallow places among the islands where only the shallowest draft boats can go.

LAUNCH SITE: The Government Dock is just off Highway 17 in the town of Spanish. From 17 turn south onto Trunk Road (at the town center). Cross the tracks and bear to the right through the first two intersections, then turn left onto Garnier Road. Drive three blocks to the marina at the end of the road.

 **DIRECTIONS**

START: From the Spanish marina paddle southwest toward **Green Island**. There are several islands shown on the accompanying map that are more like marshy sandbars, and you may have to give them a wide berth when the water is low. *Caution:* Boat traffic entering and leaving the marina must navigate through a narrow channel along the north shore of the river entrance, so be sure to cross the channel quickly and keep your distance.

MILE 1.0: After you've passed a small group of rock islands, head for the channel between Green Island and the hook-shaped peninsula just east of the island, **Black Fly Point**.

MILE 2.0: Once you reach Green Island, paddle southwest along either side of the island. Note that there are not many landing places on these islands. If you need a break, try Aird Island instead; its north shore has a very narrow gravel beach, but it may be underwater if the lake level is high.

MILE 3.5: If you are doing the 7.0-mile trip, turn at the southwestern end of Green Island and begin paddling to the northwest, around the island, and back to the marina. Green Island is not an easy place to land, so if you want a break try Aird Island instead. If you are doing the Aird

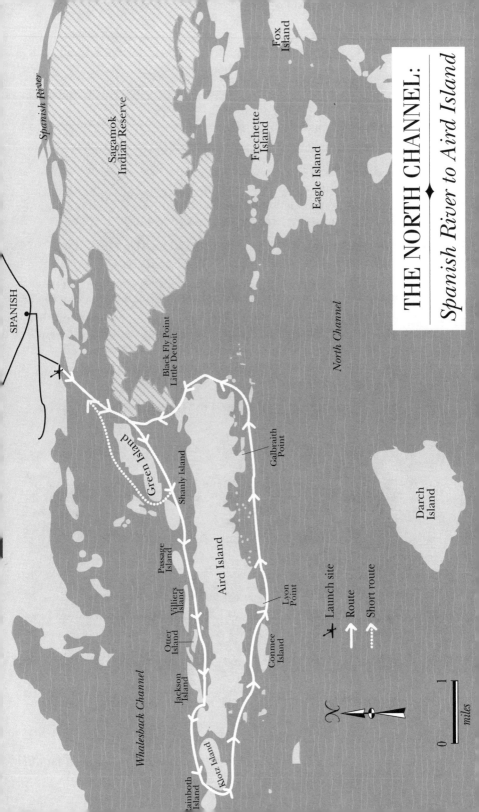

THE NORTH CHANNEL:
Spanish River to Aird Island

Spanish River

SPANISH

Sagamok
Indian Reserve

Fox
Island

Frechette
Island

Eagle Island

Black Fly Point
Little Detroit

North Channel

Green Island

Shanly Island

Galbraith
Point

Darch
Island

Passage
Island

Villiers
Island

Aird Island

Lyon
Point

Otter
Island

Jackson
Island

Conmee
Island

Whalesback Channel

Rainboth
Island

Klotz Island

✕ Launch site
⬆ Route
⋯➤ Short route

miles
0   1

Island circuit, continue paddling to the southwest, from Green to Shanly, the next island down the line.

MILE 5.0: In the middle of **Villiers Island** on the south side is a small gravel beach that makes a good picnic or rest spot.

MILE 7.0: The chain of islands intersects Aird Island, but there is enough water for paddlers to slip through the grassy channel between Aird and **Jackson Island**.

MILE 7.5: Some maps may show a channel between Aird and Klotz Islands, but it was not open when we paddled the area. Continue west to the end of **Klotz Island (N 46° 08.386', W 82° 30.469')**.

MILE 8.5: Paddle around the western tip of Klotz Island, then begin paddling eastward. The south shore of **Aird Island** consists of rocky points that alternate with shallow bays and beaches or marshes. Most of the good beaches have cabins (there are about five on this side of the island), but you should still be able to find a spot to get out and stretch. *Caution:* The next 7.0 miles have some exposure to southwesterly winds in particular, although the fetch is not enough to allow big seas to develop. Strong winds may make paddling uncomfortable, especially along the shallow areas.

MILE 11.0: Pass by **Conmee Island** and the large marsh north of it on Aird.

MILES 11.0–14.0: Thread your way through the numerous shoals and small islets. On the other side of **Lyon Point** are a few small beaches, but you may have to walk your kayak through the shallows to get to them. Also note that some of the beaches have cabins on them—please respect private property.

MILE 14.0: Just before **Galbraith Point** (count two small points east of it), there is a good beach for a break.

MILES 14.0–17.0: Make your way through more clusters of small islands, paddle around the eastern side of the island, and head north for **Little Detroit (N 46° 08.980', W 82° 22.550')**, the narrow gap between Aird Island and Black Fly Point.

MILE 17.0: Those using a topo map to navigate will notice a concentration of named landmarks around Little Detroit. This area was the site of the town of Spanish Mills, although there does not seem to be anything left today. Paddle through the gap and turn and paddle north.

MILES 18.0–20.0: Paddle by Green Island and return to the marina.

Where to Eat & Where to Stay

RESTAURANTS & LODGING There is not much in the town of Spanish, but you can call the Municipal Office at (705) 844–2565 for more information. There will be many more choices in Espanola. **CAMPING** Try **Mitchell's Camp** (705–494–3114).

Lake Huron
Georgian Bay

Georgian Bay

Georgian Bay is part of Lake Huron, but it is quite distinct in appearance and geology from the rest of the lake. Unlike larger craft, canoes and kayaks can easily paddle in water only a few inches deep, giving them access to a myriad of inlets, islets, and shallow channels.

Paddling Georgian Bay presents a challenge navigationally, at least if you are trying to find a particular spot. Make sure that you carry maps and a compass. It is hard to get completely lost because you can always find your way back by keeping the land on one side and paddling until you hit something familiar. But the low, flat islands that look so distinctive on the map are confusingly similar when viewed edge on. You will have to watch your map and heading carefully to keep track of your position if you are unfamiliar with the area.

Although the islands and shoals of Georgian Bay provide lots of quiet paddling, it is hard to plan a trip that is entirely sheltered. You will have to cross entrances to some of the larger bays that have deep channels and few islands or shoals to break up the big waves off the lake. Planning a trip early in the summer will help you avoid the winds that pick up in August and September. Whenever you are going, we recommend that you bring along a VHF weather radio. The water temperature varies quite a bit during the season; we recommend a wet suit or dry suit if paddling in the spring or fall.

A look at a nautical chart will show you that the water may be only a few feet deep miles out from shore, and although the shoals help to break up incoming waves, there are drawbacks to paddling in such shallow water. In addition, waves passing over a rock shelf or shoal will increase in height and steepness and may catch paddlers unaware if the depth changes suddenly. As you paddle along, scan the water ahead for shoals that break only intermittently with the bigger waves. If you are approaching shore from more open water, you may have to pass over the rock shelves that run along the mainland, or keep paddling until you find a safer route to land. Plan a wind day or two into your itinerary; spend the bad days on shore or exploring one of the inland channels or rivers.

The prevalence of bare rock shoreline leads to several problems for kayakers. Landing loaded kayaks on this type of shoreline can be problematic even in calm weather. Whether you unload first and then carry your boat to higher ground or vice versa, be extremely cautious of the slippery algae growing on rocks underwater. Because you will very likely be camping on bare rock, a freestanding tent does make life easier.

When choosing a camping spot, make sure that your island has enough soil on it to bury human waste 6 inches deep at a minimum distance of 100 feet (30 meters) from the water. French River Provincial Park asks you to burn or carry out toilet paper. A few of the more popular islands we visited were littered with toilet paper, and with sea kayaking and use of the area increasing, this problem is only going to get worse. With so little soil on these islands, it is especially important to practice leave-no-trace camping.

The shoreline of Georgian Bay is a mixture of Crown land, park land, Indian reserves, and patent (private) lands. Please check in with the park you are visiting for current permit and camping requirements. Indian reserve land should be treated as private land; please respect the owners' wishes and do not camp unless you have permission. Non-residents of Canada are required to pay a $10 per night fee for camping on Crown land. Permits can be purchased at any Ministry of Natural Resources office or at any store that sells hunting and fishing licenses.

Route 3:

Killarney to the French River

I think most paddlers would agree that the stretch of shoreline from Killarney Provincial Park to the historic French River is the best paddle in Georgian Bay and certainly one of the best in the Great Lakes. The scenery is wonderful, with its worn islands of shield granite and their windswept white pines. The area is an island-hoppers paradise with excellent camping. The northern shore of Georgian Bay has less road access and fewer cottages than the southern shores, and it's easy to find a quiet spot to call your own for a day or a week.

TRIP HIGHLIGHTS: Excellent scenery, classic Georgian Bay trip.

TRIP RATING:

Beginner: 8-mile round-trip from Killarney (Chickanishing River launch) to Fox Islands and back.

Intermediate/Advanced: 45-plus mile one-way trip from Killarney to Key River (round-trip distance of 100 miles).

TRIP DURATION: Day trip to overnight for beginner; five to seven days for intermediate/advanced.

NAVIGATION AIDS: CHS charts 2245 and 2244, Canadian topographic maps 41 H/14 and 41 H/15 at 1:50,000, or CHS small-craft chart 2204 (a set of four strip charts showing the shoreline from Byng Inlet to Killarney in great detail).

CAUTIONS: Intermittent exposure to southerly winds, shoals with steep or breaking waves, some boat traffic in channels.

TRIP PLANNING: The distances given earlier should be regarded as minimums. With so many islands it is difficult to travel in a straight line, and there are many possible routes from point A to B. It is probably best to plan on a somewhat leisurely pace, partly for

this reason and partly because this is not a landscape-seascape that rewards high-speed touring. Take the time to explore the byways and backwaters and don't just stick to the outer islands. Along the northern shore of Georgian Bay, most of the inlets and bays open to the south or southwest, and strong wind from these directions can bring big waves in through the deep channels. Wait for good weather before crossing these channels or going around the more exposed points.

All of the various outlets of the French River and the Bustard Islands are within the boundaries of the French River Provincial Park, and you should use the established campsites when staying there. There is a good park map showing the location of these sites. Call (705) 857-3228 for more information. Non-Canadian residents will need Crown land camping permits for staying on government land (see p. 20).

LAUNCH SITE: For the Killarney launch point, take Highway 69 from Sudbury or Parry Sound to Highway 637. Drive west on 637 to the Killarney Provincial Park Office. You will need to purchase your vehicle permits here. From the park entrance, continue 0.9 mile west on 637 to Chickanishing River Road, turn east and drive 1.0 mile to the canoe and kayak launch; the parking area is just beyond. The launch point is within the park boundaries, and you will need to purchase a $7.00/day permit for your vehicle. Alternatively you can buy a $50 annual permit, or you can get a shuttle from Killarney Outfitters. They are located very close to the Chickanishing River and provide shuttles and parking at very reasonable rates. For groups with several vehicles, this may be the cheapest way to go. For more information, contact Killarney Outfitters at (800) 287–2828.

If you are setting up your own car shuttle for a one-way trip, be warned that it will involve driving over 200 kilometers from Killarney Park to Key River and back again. It will, however, cut your paddling distance in half if you plan on doing the whole route; it may be worth doing if you are limited in time.

This route can be done in the other direction as well. There is access and parking at the Key Marine Resort (705–383–2308), located on Highway 69 just north of the bridge over the Key River. There is a daily parking fee.

DIRECTIONS

START: Paddle southeast down the **Chickanishing River** toward Georgian Bay.

MILE 0.5: At the river mouth you will see a few islands between you and the bay, but this area is somewhat exposed to southwesterly winds. Directly east of the river mouth is **Philip Edward Island**, and the channel north of the island is **Collins Inlet**. If the weather is truly awful out on the bay, you can take the extremely sheltered inlet route east to **Beaverstone Bay**. It is not recommended, however, because the walls of this channel are fairly steep, cottages have been built on most of the good landing places, and there is a fair amount of boat traffic. Moreover you will miss the better scenery on the outside. Unless you're in a real hurry, you may want to wait out bad weather. Camping is possible on the islands along the outer park shore, and no permit is needed for island sites. Continuing on, paddle southeast to **South Point**.

MILE 1.0: Pass by South Point and paddle east toward Winakaching Bay. The islands near South Point seem to be heavily used by campers.

MILE 2.5: The channel leading to **Winakaching Bay (N 45° 58.618', W 81° 23.055')** is fairly sheltered by the outside islands. This pretty spot is certainly worth a visit, with its near vertical granite walls diving into the water. You may see a sailboat or two anchored here. After you leave the islands clustered around the entrance to the bay, paddle east across a wider bay toward the **Fox Islands**.

MILES 3.5–4.0: Paddle by **Solomon Island** and continue east toward **East Fox Island (N 45° 57.517', W81° 20.734')**. Apart from the La Cloche Mountains in Killarney Park, the Fox Islands are some of the highest land along this section of shoreline. The islands closest to shore have cottages on them, but the outer islands (**West Fox** and **Martins**) make for good exploring if the weather is calm. As the land around is flatter, climbing to the top gives one a good view. *Caution:* The Fox Islands extend farther south than the islands on either side and are exposed to winds from every direction but north. In addition, many of the islands have shores of steep sloping rock, which is difficult to land on and prone to clapotis. If it is rough, better to keep some of the inner islands between you and the bay. Those whose destination is the Fox Islands can paddle back to the Chickanishing River by the same general route. Others should continue east.

MILES 5.0–6.5: Pass by **West** and then by **East Desjardins Bays**; both have plenty of islands for shelter or stopping. *Caution:* The point between East Desjardins and **Solomon Bay** is somewhat exposed to southerly winds; use caution before proceeding.

MILE 7.0: Duck behind the islands of **Big Rock Bay** and explore the channel.

MILE 8.0: The next point east of the bay is also exposed to wind and waves off the lake.

MILE 9.0: Pass **Bateman Island** (actually another point and not an island) and turn north into entrance of **Bear Bay**. *Sidetrip:* Follow Bear Bay north. See if you can find the very narrow channel that runs through **Moose Bay** and behind Deer Island and exits in Deer Island Bay. If it is rough out on the bay, this detour will provide you with some shelter.

MILES 11.0–12.5: Continue past **Deer**, **Hincks**, and **Toad Islands** into the entrance to Beaverstone Bay, a large body of water at the east end of Philip Edward Island. *Caution:* This is the other entrance to the Collins Inlet; beware of boats passing through the convoluted channel east of Toad Island (**N 45° 56.584', W 81° 12.917'**).

MILE 14.0: Paddle into **Sugar John Bay**, then southwest to exit the bay and round the next big point. *Caution:* Sugar John Bay is open to

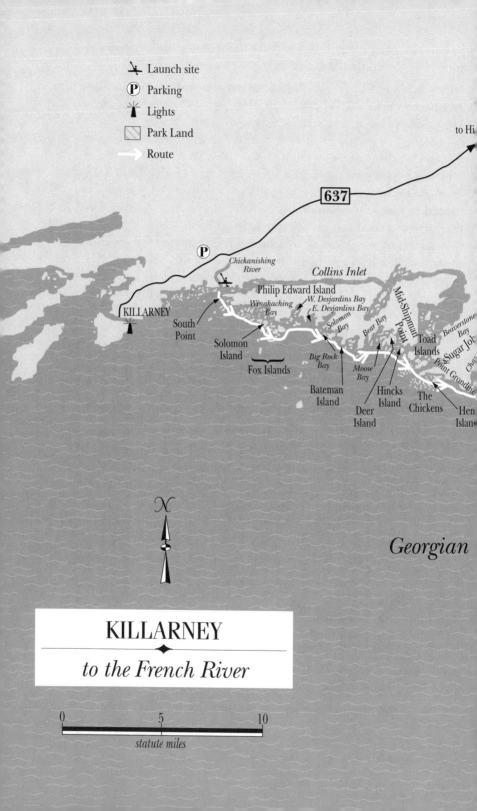

KILLARNEY
to the French River

statute miles

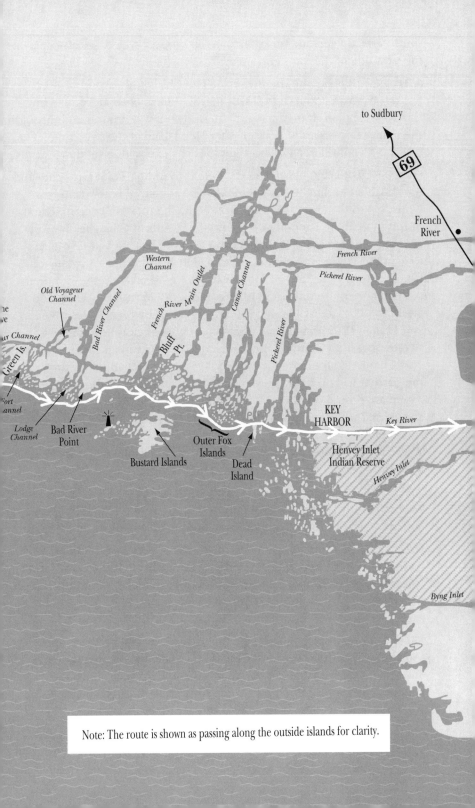

to Sudbury

69

French River

French River

Pickerel River

Western Channel

Old Voyageur Channel

French River Main Outlet

Canoe Channel

Bad River Channel

Pickerel River

...ne ...we

...ur Channel

Green Is.

...ort ...annel

Lodge Channel

Bad River Point

Bluff Pt.

Bustard Islands

Outer Fox Islands

Dead Island

KEY HARBOR

Key River

Henvey Inlet Indian Reserve

Henvey Inlet

Byng Inlet

Note: The route is shown as passing along the outside islands for clarity.

southwesterly wind and waves. Beware an especially nasty set of shoals on the west side of the bay's entrance.

MILE 14.5: Paddle into the shelter of **The Chickens**, a group of numerous small islands and shoals that should shield you from all but the worst weather. It may take time to find your way around and through the maze of tiny islands. After passing **Hen Island** at the east end of The Chickens, you will need to cross another bay exposed to southerly winds.

MILES 17.0–20.0: *Caution:* Use care when rounding **Point Grondine** and the shoals extending to the southeast. The stretch of water from Point Grondine to the entrance of the Voyageur Channel can be a minefield in rough weather. Paddling deep into the islands of **Chaughis Bay** will give you only temporary relief because you will have to paddle out again to gain the Voyageur Channel. *Sidetrip:* Batt Bay and the Voyageur Channel (N 45° 56.337', W 81° 04.940') are extremely pretty, with their parallel lines of humpbacked islands and windblown pines. Once you are in the Voyageur Channel, you are entering the French River System and French River Provincial Park. Paddling northeast through the shallow grassy area and up the Voyageur Channel will take you across the Fort Channel and eventually to the Old Voyageur Channel. At this point the current will probably prevent you from going any farther upstream. There are several small rapids just upstream where the river is constricted within a narrow rock channel. Return to the lake via the Fort Channel. Total distance for this sidetrip is about 3.5 miles. *Caution:* There is a fair amount of boat traffic in the French River System, and motorboats even go up and down the rapids. Be sure to stay out of their way.

MILE 20.0: If you are taking the outside route, continue paddling east. You are now within the boundaries of French River Provincial Park.

MILE 21.0: To avoid going around the outside of **Eagle Nest Point**, paddle northwest into Batt Bay and pick a way through the islands until you reach **Green Island**. If you can, find the channel at the south end of Green Island or paddle around the outside. *Caution:* Another set of extensive shoals lies just off the southern end of Green Island.

MILE 23.0: *Caution:* The Fort Channel is also extremely exposed to southerly wind and waves, and should be avoided in rough weather: Take the Voyageur Channel if conditions are bad. Once across the channel you can duck behind islands and zigzag through channels if you want quieter water.

Killarney to the French River

MILE 25.5: The **Lodge Channel** is another outlet of the French River, part of a larger branch called the **Bad River Channel (N 45° 54.816', W80° 59.029')**. This time there are plenty of islands in the channel. There is a marina about 1.0 mile upstream—this is one of the major routes for sailboats and motorboats, so keep an eye out for traffic when crossing the Lodge and Bad River Channels. If you want to paddle upstream (don't try this in high water), you should portage around the rapids upstream of the channel entrance. The rapids and portages are marked on the park map.

MILE 27.0: About 1.0 mile east of the Bad River Channel, you will run out of islands and round a point. You are now in the Fingerboards, another set of shoals. *Caution:* Avoid the Fingerboards in heavy seas.

MILES 27.0–29.0: Once around the point you will have the choice of paddling on the outside or winding your way through a series of islands until you reach the **Main Outlet**.

MILE 29.0: *Caution:* The entrance to the Main Outlet is open to wind and waves from the southwest, and there will be some boat traffic as well. Use caution when crossing the entrance. *Sidetrip:* The **Bustard Islands** (see Rte. 4) are less than 1.0 mile from the islands around Cantin Point. Although the crossing is a short one, it is better to leave from the deeper water of the Main Outlet than the islands and shoals around Cantin Point. The water is only a few feet deep and will be tricky to negotiate in rough weather.

MILES 30.5–33.5: Once across the Main Outlet, you have a choice of continuing east on the outside of the islands or taking the small craft channel. The inside channel is very pretty and sheltered, but it may have a fair amount of motor traffic. If it's rough on the outside, this is an easy choice, but otherwise it's your call. Either way you will end up at the **Outer Fox Islands**, another little archipelago. Just north of the islands is **Fox Bay**, which has the last set of campsites within the French River Park boundaries. As you leave the park and approach **Key Harbour**, it will become more difficult to find good places to camp as the number of cottages and the amount of boat traffic increase. Continue paddling east toward **Dead Island**.

MILE 37.0: There is a picnic site on the northeast side of Dead Island. The island was a native burial ground. After you leave Dead Island, you will pass the **Pickerel River**, which marks the eastern boundary of French River Provincial Park.

Killarney to the French River

The French River &
the Voyageurs

The French River is divided into four main outlets: the Pickerel River, Main Outlet, Bad River, and Western Outlet. Each of the four is subdivided into more channels. The river originates from Lake Nipissing and is also fed by several tributary rivers, such as the Pickerel River, resulting in a maze of waterways leading from the lake to Georgian Bay. The French River was part of the Voyageurs canoe route from Montreal to Grand Portage or Fort William at the northwestern end of Lake Superior. There the 36-foot-long *canots de maitre* would meet the smaller north canoes, which were bringing furs from as far away as Lake Athabasca. Trade goods and supplies from Montreal were exchanged for furs at the annual Rendez-Vous, quite the wild party by all accounts. Apparently there is some dispute as to which particular channel the Voyageurs used, but in any case as you paddle the French River, you will be traveling in the same river and seeing much the same scenery as they did more than two hundred years ago.

MILE 38.5: Continue paddling east toward the entrance to Key Harbour. There are a number of cottages visible near the mouth of the **Key River**.

MILES 40.0–45.0: Paddle up the river to Highway 69. The river had very little current when we were there, but it may be a different matter at high water (if you are paddling early in the year, you may want to do the trip in the opposite direction). The river is pretty, with gray granite walls and grassy bays, but there will be motorboat traffic on it. Please stay clear of the channel marked by buoys. The south shore is part of the **Henvey Inlet Indian Reserve**, and there is no landing or camping without permission. The north shore is mostly Crown land, but good landing places are not plentiful. At Mile 45.0 The Key Marine Resort is just east of Highway 69 on the north side of the river. There are boat ramps, showers, a small store, and lodging available.

RESTAURANTS At the Key River end of the route, the **Key Marine Resort** has a restaurant. Call (705) 383–2308 for more information. On the Killarney side, try the **Sportsman's Inn** (705–287–2411) in the main part of town. There are also a couple of small take-out food booths at the marinas, including a fish and chips shop at the town docks at the end of Highway 637.

LODGING In Killarney there are three main options: the Sportsman's Inn (see "Restaurants"), the **Killarney Bay Inn** (705–287–2011), or the **Killarney Mountain Lodge** (800–461–1117). This tiny town is overwhelmed with visitors in the summer, and reservations are highly recommended. The Key Marine Resort has cottages available for rental (see "Restaurants"). **CAMPING** **Killarney Provincial Park** has a large campground located just off Highway 637 at George Lake. This park is extremely popular and reservations are essential. Call (705) 287–2800 for reservations, or (705) 287–2900 for general information about the park. The **Rogue's Marina** in Killarney has tent camping available; call (705) 287–9900 for more information. The **Key Marine Resort** also has camping available. **Grundy Lake Provincial Park** is located off Highway 69 not far from the Key River. Call (705) 383–2369 for more information.

Route 4:

The Bustard Islands

The Bustard Islands have an awkward name but don't be fooled: They are extremely pretty and make a good choice of destination for those who want to see the scenery of the north shore of Georgian Bay without doing the longer trip from Killarney to the Key River. (They can also be added on to Rte. 3 and are well worth the detour if you have the time.)

TRIP HIGHLIGHTS: Excellent scenery, beautiful island group.

TRIP RATING:

Intermediate: 39-mile paddle down the Key River to the Bustards and back.

TRIP DURATION: Two to four days.

NAVIGATION AIDS: CHS chart 2244, Canadian topographic map: *Key Harbor* (41 H/15) at 1:50,000.

CAUTIONS: Boat traffic, exposed crossing, extensive shoals.

TRIP PLANNING: The only drawback to the Bustards is the lack of campsites. They are part of French River Provincial Park and camping is permitted in designated sites only. (There is a map for the French River Provincial Park showing the location of campsites within the park. Call 705–857–3228 for information.) There are only two sites on the islands, available on a first-come, first-served basis, and they are usually taken. There are, however, six sites around the Main Outlet of the French River (and more around Fox Island to the east) that are within easy distance of the Bustards. It is not difficult to camp on the mainland and do a day trip to and around the islands.

The route description is for a trip going from Key Harbour to the southern tip of Dead Island, then crossing straight west from there to the Bustards. On a good day, this is the fastest way to go, but if the weather is iffy, it is more prudent to paddle along the mainland and cross from the vicinity of the main outlet of the French River, only 1 mile at the shortest point. (See Miles 29.0–45.0, Rte. 3 for details of the land route.)

LAUNCH SITE: The Key River and Highway 69 intersect south of Sudbury. On the north side of the river is the Key Marine Resort, which has boat ramps and parking available for a fee. Rest rooms are available near the put in. Launch from here.

DIRECTIONS

START: From the Key Marine Resort, paddle west down the **Key River**. The boat channel down the river is marked with buoys; please stay clear of the channel while paddling.

MILES 1.0–8.0: There are no rapids on this section of the river, and it is a leisurely paddle down the river to **Key Harbour**. The southern bank of the river is part of the **Henvey Inlet Indian Reserve**, while the northern shore is mostly Crown land, with a few cottages here and there. The river has sections of steep granite cliffs that alternate with grassy bays.

MILES 8.0–10.0: Paddle out of the river and into Key Harbour, a small village at the mouth of the river. Continue paddling due west, past the

The Bustard Islands

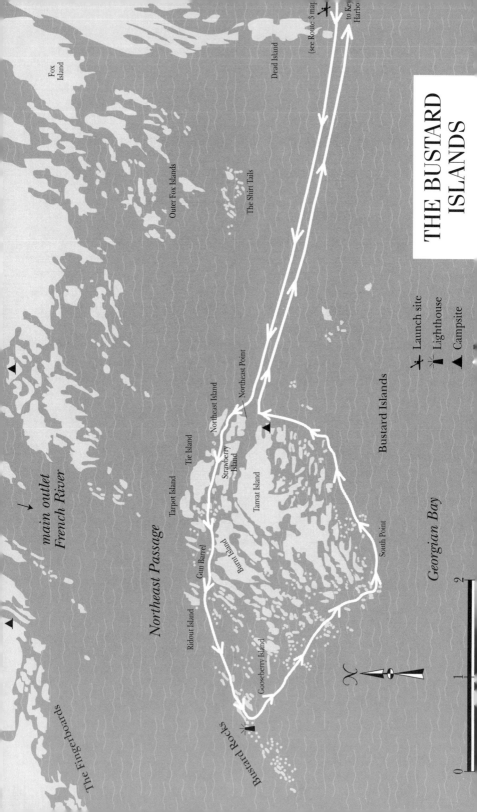

THE BUSTARD ISLANDS

- ✈ Launch site
- ※ Lighthouse
- ▲ Campsite

main outlet French River

The Fingerboards

Fox Island

Outer Fox Islands

Northeast Passage

Ridout Island

Tarpot Island

Tie Island

Gun Barrel

Burnt Island

Northeast Island

Strawberry Island

Tamrat Island

Northeast Point

The Shirt Tails

Dead Island

to Key Harbor

(see Route 3 map)

Bustard Rocks

Gooseberry Island

South Point

Bustard Islands

Georgian Bay

0   1   2

islands and shoals to the south, heading toward the southern tip of **Dead Island**. *Caution:* As you leave Key Harbour, you will be exposed to wind and waves from the west.

MILE 11.5: Dead Island marks the eastern boundary of French River Provincial Park. There is a picnic area on its northeast side. *Caution:* After you leave Dead Island, you will lose the protection of the shoals and islands south of Key Harbour; use caution if southerly winds are forecast.

MILES 11.5–15.5: You will pass by some shoals east of Dead Island and south of **The Shirt Tails**. Continue toward **Northeast Point**.

MILE 15.5: Once at the northeast corner of the island group, you can decide which way to circumnavigate the islands, depending on the weather. Directions are given here for the counterclockwise direction. Paddle west between **Strawberry** and **Tie Islands**.

MILE 16.5: You will enter a harbor with small islands scattered around, the site of several fish camps before the invasion of the sea lamprey. There are a few cabins here, and it seems to be a very popular anchorage for motorboats and sailboats. Paddle west and out of the harbor.

MILE 17.0: You are now in the **Gun Barrel**, a channel that runs west out into the open lake. *Caution:* Don't attempt the next leg of the trip unless you have fair weather. The outer islands are exposed to southerly and westerly winds; negotiating the shoals in big waves is very difficult. Paddle west-southwest toward the Bustard Rocks.

MILE 19.0: The largest of the **Bustard Rocks (N 45° 53.442', W 80° 57.152')** has three standard-issue red and white lights. This is a tough place to land even on a calm day because the rock is steep. Once on the island it is a short walk down to the end of the rock. You might sympathize with the lightkeeper who, apparently feeling somewhat claustrophobic during his time there, tried to liven things up by bringing over good soil to garden in. The garden and soil are long gone, and only a few small plants manage to hold on now. From the Bustard Rocks, paddle southeast back toward the main island group.

MILES 20.5–21.0: Between **Burnt Island** and **Tanvat Island**, there is the entrance to a narrow, winding **channel (N 45° 52.723', W 80° 55.473')**. *Sidetrip:* At some point on your trip, you may want to paddle northeast through this channel. It's very pretty and sheltered. There is a marshy spot near Strawberry Island; depending on the water level, you may not be able to get all the way through to Northeast Point (you should still be able to turn north and get to **Tarpot Island**, however). Once past the entrance to the channel, continue paddling southeast toward South Point. *Caution:* The area around South Point is the most exposed on this trip. Wait for good weather before trying it. You can paddle behind the islands just south of Tanvat to gain some shelter. This is a very pleasant spot to lunch provided the weather cooperates. Turn and paddle to the northeast, following the shore of Tanvat Island.

MILES 21.0–23.0: This section of shoreline is a maze of bays and islands. Make sure to detour into the bays and explore a little. One of the bays we visited had many small, rounded islands, each with bent white pine, looking like a flotilla of sailboats. You may find blueberries in season around the shores. There is a campsite on one of the outermost islands.

MILE 23.5: You are back at Northeast Point.

MILES 23.5–39.0: Return to Key Harbour the same way you came.

Where to Eat & Where to Stay

RESTAURANTS The **Key Marine Resort** has a restaurant at the launch point (705–383–2308), and there are several roadside diners along Highway 69 between the Key River and Sudbury. **LODGING** A few miles north of the Key River is the French River, with a few motels right on Highway 69. Try the **French River Inn** (705–857–2788). **CAMPING** **Grundy Lake Provincial Park** is located off Highway 69, not far from the Key River. Call (705) 383–2369 for more information.

Route 5:

━ ━ ━ ━ ━ ━ ━ ━ ━ ━ ━ ━ ━ ━ ⟶

Byng Inlet to Bayfield Inlet

The length and easy access at both ends of the Byng-Bayfield route make it a good weekend trip. Although there are some cottages along this route, there are still enough islands and bays to find a quiet spot in the backwaters.

TRIP HIGHLIGHTS: Good scenery, camping.

TRIP RATING:
Beginner: 4–6 mile trip around the islands of Bayfield Inlet.
Beginner/Intermediate: 18-mile, one-way trip from Byng Inlet to Bayfield Inlet, or 36-mile round-trip.

TRIP DURATION: Part day to three days.

NAVIGATION AIDS: CHS chart 2243, Canadian topographic maps 41 H/15 and 41 H/10 at 1:50,000.

CAUTIONS: Some exposure to south and west winds, extensive shoals, boat traffic.

TRIP PLANNING: Beginning paddlers doing the longer trip should plan to go early in the summer before the winds pick up because there are a few spots along the route where paddlers are exposed to wind and waves off the bay. Your trip will probably be more enjoyable if you avoid holiday weekends; if possible paddle on a weekday to avoid the heavier boat traffic.

There are no parks or Indian reserves along this section of shore; it is mostly Crown land with a small amount of patent land. Non-Canadian residents will need to purchase Crown land camping permits (see p. 20).

LAUNCH SITES: You may launch from either Britt on Byng Inlet or from Bayfield Harbour. To reach Bayfield Harbour, go north on

Highway 69 from Point Au Baril Station and drive about 1.0 mile to the Highway 529 exit. Go north on 529 for 4.2 miles. Turn west onto 529A and drive another 2.8 miles to a government dock and a parking area on the left. Parking is limited, and if the lot next to the ramp is full, try the Hangdog Marina west of the government launch. There are no fees for launching or parking at the government dock. If you are doing an out-and-back trip, Bayfield Harbor is the more convenient launch spot.

To get to Britt, take Highway 69 north to the Highway 526 exit (to Britt) and drive south/west for 2.9 miles to a government dock. There is no fee to use this facility, but there is no public lot here. You will have to park at the pay lot another 0.1 mile west of the launch (across from St. Amants store) and pay for parking in the store. Alternatively, there is a full-service marina another 1.0 mile west (Wright's Marina).

DIRECTIONS

START: Start at Britt and paddle west past **Old Mill Island** (the site of a sawmill during Byng Inlet's lumbertown days) and **Rabbit Island** toward the end of Byng Inlet. *Caution:* Byng Inlet is fairly narrow, but it gets quite a bit of boat traffic. Stay out of boats' way as much as possible.

MILE 1.5: Look for the wreck of the *Northern Belle*, which burned in Byng Inlet in the late nineteenth century. It is in about 5–10 feet of water.

MILES 2.5–4.0: As you come to the end of Byng Inlet, bear to the left and enter the south channel below Clark Island, then head for the first channel between the outer islands and the mainland. *Caution:* Strong westerly winds may make this an uncomfortable place to be. There is a deep channel leading out to the bay that may allow bigger waves to get past the shoals. As the Byng Inlet is also the outlet of the Magnetawan River, the river's current at high water may also create choppy conditions at its mouth.

MILES 4.0–6.0: Even if you paddle behind the islands near the entrance to the south channel, you will have to come out again to get around **Gerry Island**—unless you want to portage across it. *Caution:* The southwest tip of Gerry Island is open to the bay.

MILES 6.0–8.5: Once around, continue paddling south past **Burritts Bay**. After you reach the point that forms the southern shore of this bay, you have a choice of continuing along the outside or paddling east and south into Norgate Inlet, which runs through and behind the islands next to the mainland. Take the outside route only if the lake is calm. There are some cottages on the outermost of the two parallel channels.

MILE 8.5: Either way, you'll end up inside the **Norgate Inlet (N 45° 42.175', W 80° 36.759')**.

MILES 8.5–11.0: The recesses of **Kenrick Bay** are shallow and grassy, but the line of islands that runs between Kenrick and Prisque Bay is very nice, though you'll find a few cottages on the islands. If you follow the islands south, you will run into the mainland; if you turn and follow it to the southwest, you'll find the channel between the mainland and Foster Island, which leads to the **Mud Channel (N 45° 40.741', W 80° 36.759')**.

MILES 11.0–12.5: Paddle south past the Mud Channel and continue along the side of **Olwyn Island** until you reach the **North Channel of the Naiscoot River (N 45° 38.038', W 80° 35.644')**. *Sidetrip:* There are many possible sidetrips in the Naiscoot River, which is split into three different channels, each with islands and bays. Take some time to poke around if you're not in a hurry.

MILES 12.5–14.5: Unless you're taking the long detour up the Naiscoot River, continue paddling southeast. *Caution:* The next section is both very shallow and open to the lake. If it is very rough, you may want to stay well out from shore and take the marked channel into the Alexander Passage at Mile 14.5. When you reach the entrance to the **Alexander Passage (N 45° 38.038', W 80° 34.162')** turn and paddle southeast into the passage. The concentration of cottages will increase again as you approach Bayfield Harbour.

MILE 16.0: Once past **Meneilly Island**, the passage opens out into an island-filled bay. Although there are number of cottages around, this is still a very pretty place and worth making a detour to paddle around a little. When you're done, continue heading east toward the Bayfield dock (unless you're returning to Byng Inlet, in which case you should paddle back by the same route).

MILE 18.5: The government dock and parking area is on the north side of Bayfield Harbour.

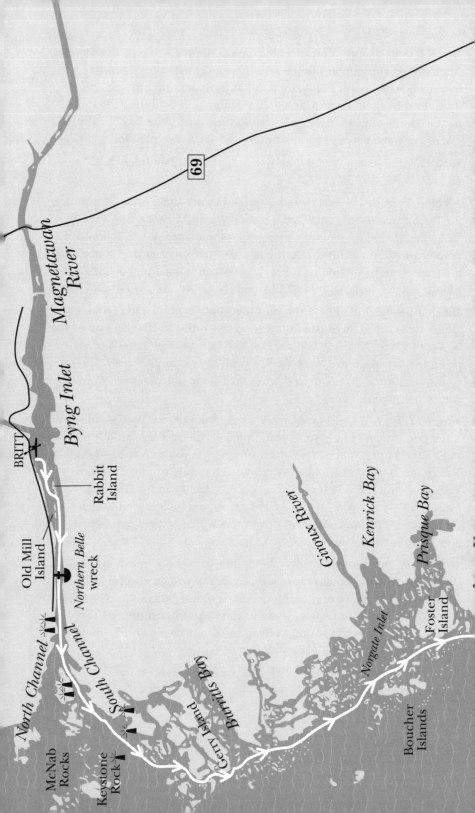

Note: The route is shown as passing along the outside islands and shoals for clarity.

BYNG INLET

to Bayfield Inlet

BAYFIELD

to Highway 69

Bayfield Harbour

Naiscoot River
Middle Channel
South Channel

Charles Inlet

Alexander Passage

Oldham Point

Meneilly Island

h Channel

⊁ Launch site
⚓ Lighthouse
⚓ Shipwreck
⇧ Route

0   1   2   3
statute miles

Where to Eat & Where to Stay

RESTAURANTS & LODGING For a list of accommodations and local restaurants, call the Parry Sound Chamber of Commerce at (800) 461–4261 or the Rainbow Country Travel association at (800) 465–6655.

CAMPING There are three provincial parks near Britt and Bayfield Inlet. **Grundy Lake** (705–383–2369), **Sturgeon Bay** (705–366–2521), and **Killbear Provincial Park** (705–342–5492). A number of resorts in the area offer camping as well. Call the tourist information numbers above for a list.

Route 6:

━ ━ ━ ━ ━ ━ ━ ━ ━ ━ ━ ━ ━ ━ ➤

The Mink & McCoy Island Groups

The Mink and McCoy Island groups form an arc off the
eastern shoreline of Georgian Bay just north of Parry
Sound. Paddling the arc seems to be a fairly popular trip
with kayakers, and it is a good one for paddlers who don't
have time to do a longer one. The scenery is typical
Georgian Bay, and the line of islands can be done as part of
a loop rather than an out-and-back trip. Another nifty
weekend tour with a wonderful set of islands and good
camping.

TRIP HIGHLIGHTS: Good scenery, camping.

TRIP RATING:
Beginner: 16-mile round-trip from Dillon's Cove to the McCoy
Islands and back.
Intermediate: 23-mile loop from Dillon's Cove to the McCoy and
Mink Islands and back to Dillon's Cove via Franklin Island.

TRIP DURATION: Two to three days.

NAVIGATION AIDS: CHS chart 2243, Canadian topographic map:
Parry Sound (41 H/8 & 41 H/7) at 1:50,000.

CAUTIONS: Some boat traffic, crossing to McCoys exposed to
south/southeasterly winds and waves.

TRIP PLANNING: This is a pretty easy trip with lots of options for
detours and extensions. The only thing to beware of is strong
southerly winds and waves that can funnel up the Shawnaga Inlet,
which is relatively deep compared with the shallow areas on either
side. Planning your trip for early in the season will help you avoid
the windier weather of late summer and fall, but it would still be
wise to include a wind day in your itinerary even if you are
planning an overnight trip. The extra day can be used to explore

some of the other islands in the area if you have good weather. The islands visited on this trip are a mix of patent and private lands (but no Indian Reserve or park lands). The only permits needed are for non-Canadian citizens for Crown land camping (see introduction to Georgian Bay for information on permits).

LAUNCH SITE: The best place to launch from is Dillon's Cove, which has a government dock and ramp. There is public parking nearby, although space is limited. From Highway 69 north of Nobel, take Highway 559 west for 6.4 miles, where 559 makes a sharp turn to the left. Continue straight on Dillon Road for another 4.6 miles to the boat launch. There is a portable toilet but little else in the way of facilities. The boat launch is busy, but there is a grassy area to one side of the ramp that can be used to load kayaks before carrying them down to the water.

DIRECTIONS

START: Paddle out of **Dillon's Cove (N 45° 25.547' W 80° 19.517')** and turn west at the entrance into Shebeshekong Bay.

MILES 1.0–3.0: Paddle west past the entrance to **Sand Bay** and toward Fairhead Island. At Mile 3.0, **Fairhead Island (N 45° 26.176', W 80° 24.516')**, turn left and paddle north between the mainland and a short string of islands running parallel to it. You can also paddle directly from Fairhead to Big McCoy Island, but by curving slightly northward, you have more landing opportunites and only short jumps between islands.

MILE 4.0: When you reach the last island, turn and paddle west toward **Twin Sisters Island**. *Caution:* You are now in the **Shawnaga Inlet**, which is fairly deep and open to the south. Wait for good weather before attempting to cross. There is less fetch to the north, but even so a strong northerly wind can make things very uncomfortable.

MILES 5.0–7.5: Paddle past the northern tip of **Twin Sisters Island** and on toward the cluster of islands just south of Hertzberg Island. There are cabins on some of the islands here, but other islands are empty and can be used for a break. Continue west through this island group and paddle to Big McCoy Island.

MILE 8.0: Big McCoy Island (N 45° 27.082', W 80° 28.275') is a good place to camp: Unlike many islands in the area, it is level instead of

The Mink & McCoy Island Groups

rounded, making it a good place to set up tents. The trick is finding a spot to land as the perimeter is fairly steep. Choose the lee side of the island to land on. Take some time to explore the group of islands. If this is your final "going out" destination, return to Dillon's Cove by the same route. If you are doing the loop, turn and paddle south from Big McCoy Island, picking a way between the islets and shoals to the south.

MILE 9.0: **Birnie Island** is the last island before a gap in the chain: There is also a deeper channel between Birnie and Garland Islands—wait for good weather before crossing (there are a number of small islands around Birnie that can be used for a break). Birnie seems to have a number of osprey or other bird nests in the dead trees on the islands. We weren't there during nesting season, but if you find the nests are in use, please don't disturb the birds.

MILES 10.0–13.0: After **Garland** and **Elmtree Islands**, turn and follow the islands as they curve away to the southeast. The islands between here and the Minks are marginal for camping, especially for large groups, because they are small and have very little soil or vegetation. They are, however, free of cottages until Boucher Island.

MILES 13.0–14.0: From **Boucher** through **Stalker Islands**, the concentration of cottages increases steadily: Camping here will be tough. The west side of Stalker is empty, but as with the McCoy Islands, the

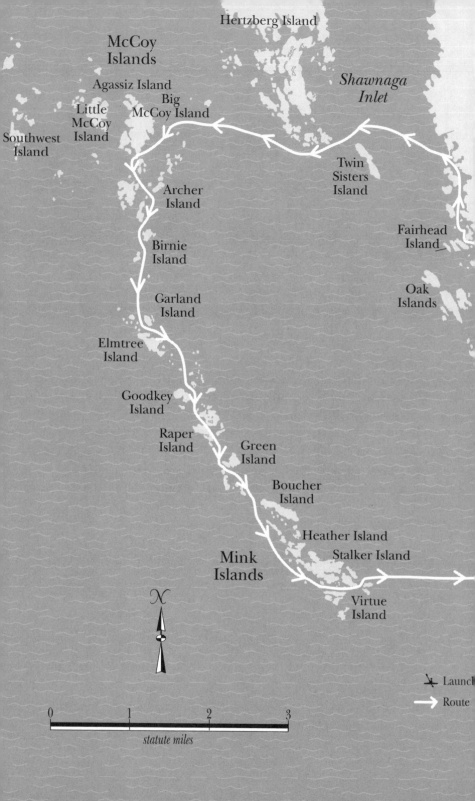

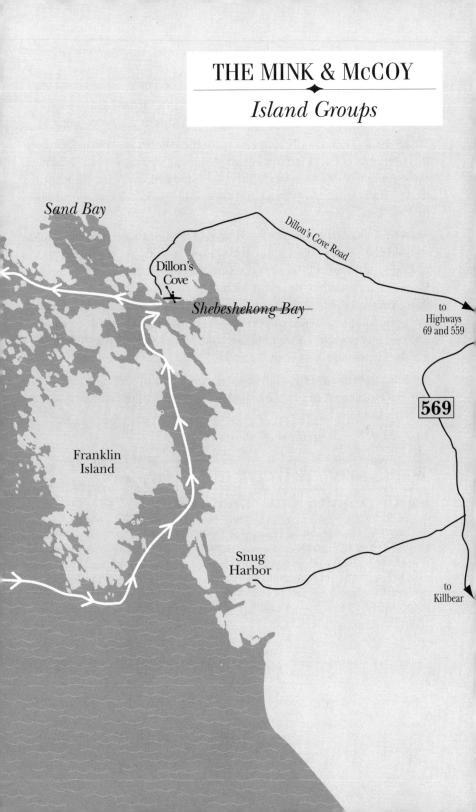

THE MINK & McCOY

Island Groups

Sand Bay

Dillon's Cove Road

Dillon's Cove

Shebeshekong Bay

to Highways 69 and 559

569

Franklin Island

Snug Harbor

to Killbear

shore consists of a 4-foot-high wall facing west, making this a poor place to paddle in rough weather and an easy place to get windbound. Choose a path through the islands, working your way to the eastern end of the **Mink Islands**. The channel between Stalker and **Virtue Islands (N 45° 22.450', W 80° 24.609')** makes a good place to start your crossing.

MILES 14.0–17.5: Paddle due east from the eastern end of the Minks to the southern end of **Franklin Island**. *Caution:* Once again you must cross the entrance to the Shawnaga Inlet, this time with even less protection from islands and shoals than before (see Mile 4.0). Use caution when making this crossing.

MILES 17.5–22.0: At the southern tip of Franklin Island, you must make a choice between paddling north along the west shore or the east shore of Franklin Island. The west shore is undeveloped but more exposed to wind and waves, while the channel on the eastern side of the island is more protected, but it faces a continuous line of vacation cottages on the mainland, with fewer opportunities for privacy. The western route will be more pleasant if weather allows it. Either way, turn and paddle north. The distance is about the same.

MILE 22.0: Whichever route you take, you'll end up near the northernmost part of Franklin Island. Turn and paddle eastward toward Dillon's Cove.

MILE 23.0: Finish up back at Dillon's Cove.

Where to Eat & Where to Stay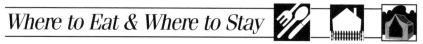

RESTAURANTS & LODGING   For a list of accommodations and local restaurants, call the Parry Sound Chamber of Commerce at (800) 461–4261 or the Rainbow Country Travel association at (800) 465–6655. **CAMPING**   **Killbear Provincial Park** is located only a few miles from Dillon's Cove. The park is a popular one, however, and reservations are recommended. Call (705) 342–5227 for reservations or (705) 342–5492 for more information. There are a number of resorts in the area that also offer camping; contact the Parry Sound Chamber of Commerce for a list of resorts.

The Mink & McCoy Island Groups

Route 7:

━ ▬ ▬ ━ ▬ ━ ▬ ━ ▬ ▬ ━ ▬ ━ ▬ ━ ▬ ➡

The Massasauga

The Massasauga, a recently created provincial park, is a
mix of inland lakes and bayside islands that offers easy
access and convenient camping for paddlers who want a
shorter trip or a sheltered paddle away from the open lake.
Because most of the park islands are so sheltered, this trip
makes a good late season trip (provided you are prepared
for cold weather and water). Paddling in the off season will
help you avoid some of the heavy boat traffic in certain
areas of the park. The scenery is very pleasant with rock
islands and mixed forest and less of the extremely
weathered rock seen in the more exposed areas of
Georgian Bay.

TRIP HIGHLIGHTS: Good scenery, camping.

TRIP RATING:
  Beginner: 17-mile loop around Moon Island.

TRIP DURATION: Two to three days.

NAVIGATION AIDS: CHS charts 2284, 2289; Canadian topographic
  map: *San Souci* (41 H/1); or the official park map (see Trip
  Planning).

CAUTIONS: Some boat traffic.

TRIP PLANNING: Like Beausoleil Island (Rte. 8), The Massasauga
  has a mixture of park and patent lands, with cottages scattered
  through the islands. Camping is allowed in designated areas only,
  and these areas are shown on the park map, sold at both The
  Massasauga and Oastler Lake Provincial Park offices. At about $10,
  this map is probably your best choice because no single topo map
  or chart provides complete coverage of the park or shows the
  campsite locations. Permits are required for camping and can also

be picked up at either park office. You will need to give your choice of campsite numbers when getting your permit, so you will need a rough idea of your itinerary and the areas you want to camp in. If you're looking for peace and quiet, it would be best to stay away from the entire east side of Moon Island, which seems to have a lot of motorboat traffic. The park itself can be busy during the peak season (Victoria Day through Labor Day), and reservations are recommended. Call (705) 378–2401 for more information and reservations.

LAUNCH SITE: The best access for kayakers is from the Pete's Place Access Point, as the other access point involves portaging to get to Georgian Bay. To get to Pete's Place, take Highway 69 to Highway 612 and drive south on 612 for 2.7 miles. Turn west onto Healy Lake Road and drive another 11.2 miles to the park entrance on the north side of the road. Pete's Place Access Point is another 0.5 miles from the turnoff. Pete's Place has pit toilets, a park office where permits are issued, parking, and a boat ramp for launching. Please note that there is no day-use parking at Pete's Place; parking is for campers only.

DIRECTIONS

START: Launch from the boat ramp at **Pete's Place** and paddle west toward the channel leading from **Blackstone Harbour** to Woods Bay.

MILE 1.0: Paddle out through the narrow connecting channel. *Caution:* Keep an eye out for motorboats, which also use the channel. Once through, paddle across **Woods Bay** to the east side of **Moon Island**. *Caution:* There is a lot of motorized traffic in Woods Bay, so use caution when crossing to Moon Island.

MILE 2.0: Once you are across, turn and paddle south toward the channel between Moon Island and the mainland.

MILE 2.5: Begin turning to the west and enter the channel. This is an extremely pretty stretch, with smooth gray granite along the side of the channel. There are a number of campsites along the shores here.

MILES 3.5–5.5: After exiting the channel, turn and begin paddling to the northwest, toward **Pleasant** and **Sharpe Islands**. Several of the larger islands along the way are park land and can be used to take a break.

MILES 5.5–6.5: The harbor formed by Sharpe Island to the north and a cluster of smaller islands to the south is another very attractive place. Campsites here may be hard to get, but they are worth trying for. Even if you are not staying here, take a detour through the harbor and out through a tiny gap on the west side (the park map shows two possible gaps, but only the southern gap was deep enough to use). Follow the channel as it turns to the southeast, and then turn to the north as soon as you get a chance.

MILES 6.5–8.0: Pass between Sharpe Island and the smaller island just west of it, then continue paddling north toward the western arm of Moon Island. *Sidetrip:* To the west of Coltman Island is Wreck Island, which makes a good break or lunch destination. There is a short trail with a self-guided tour pointing out a number of geological features of the area on the west end of the island. *Caution:* This would not be a good trip to do on a day with strong westerlies, however, because Wreck Island is more exposed to wind and waves than the rest of the trip.

MILES 8.0–11.0: Hug the shore of the westernmost tip of Moon Island and follow it as it bends to the east, then paddle northeast along the shore of **Barnyard Island** and cross to the northern side of Moon. Paddle eastward along the northern side of Moon. At Mile 11.0 turn into the channel between the east side of Moon Island and the mainland and paddle to the southeast. *Caution:* Once again you are entering a busy channel, so watch out for motorboat traffic.

MILES 11.5–12.5: To avoid some of the traffic, paddle to the west of **Miron Island**, then turn east and paddle along the south side, and then turn and go due south, aiming for **Coon Gap.**

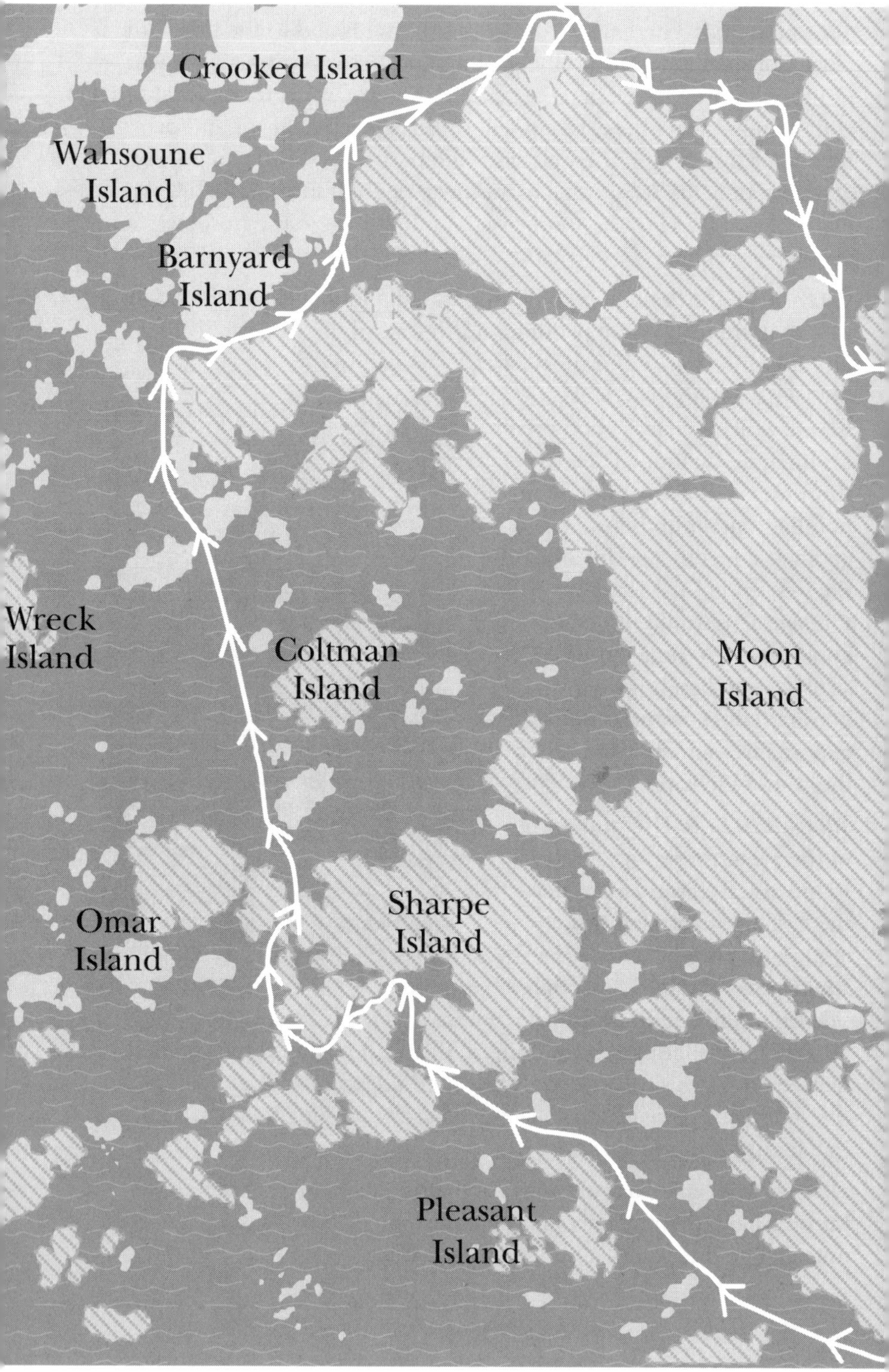

Crooked Island

Wahsoune
Island

Barnyard
Island

Wreck
Island

Coltman
Island

Moon
Island

Omar
Island

Sharpe
Island

Pleasant
Island

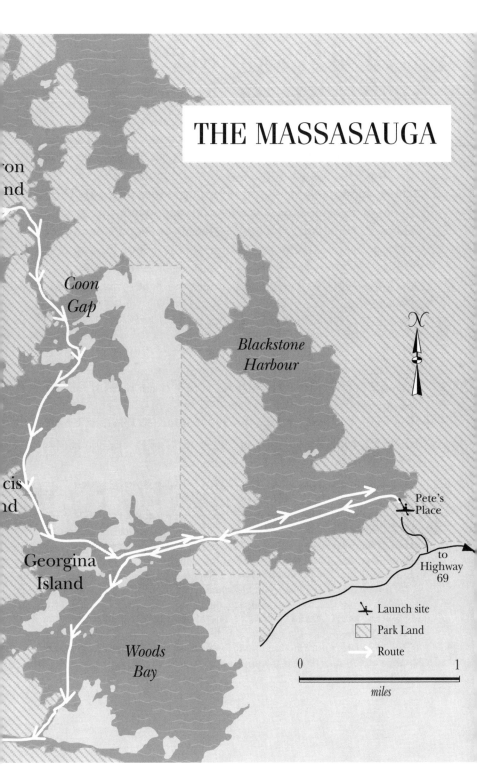

THE MASSASAUGA

Coon Gap

Blackstone Harbour

Woods Bay

Georgina Island

Pete's Place

to Highway 69

Launch site

Park Land

Route

0   1

miles

The Massasauga Rattlesnake

Parts of southern Ontario are still home to the massasauga, a small rattlesnake with a limited range in Canada (also found on the Bruce Peninsula). The snake is found in the park, but it is a rather shy and retiring snake, according to the park staff. The rattles on the end of its tail make a buzzing sound when it is alarmed. Apparently sightings are fairly rare, but if you do see or hear one, make sure not to approach or irritate the snake. Unlike most nonvenomous snakes, which have oval heads, rattlesnakes have triangular heads and saddlelike markings along their backs.

MILES 12.5–14.5: The land to the west is patent land and heavily cottaged, but Moon Island is still park land and can be used for a break. Continue south toward **Francis Island**. When you reach Francis Island, paddle east past Georgina Island to the entrance to Blackstone Harbour.

MILES 14.5–17.0: Paddle through the channel to Blackstone Harbour and return to the Pete's Place Access Point.

Where to Eat & Where to Stay

RESTAURANTS & LODGING Most of the restaurants and hotels/motels will be located near Parry Sound. Call the Parry Sound Chamber of Commerce at (800) 461–4261 for information. One thrifty and interesting option is staying at the **Park Staff House** at Pete's Place Access Point. Single rooms can be reserved at $10/person/night. Lodging is hostel style, and you must bring your own bedroll. Call the staff house manager at (705) 378–2401 for information and reservations. **CAMPING** The Massasauga has no car camping, but **Oastler Lake Provincial Park** does. It is located just south of Parry Sound. Call (705) 378–2401 for information about the park or reservations. The Parry Sound Chamber of Commerce also puts out a list of private campgrounds and resorts. Contact them for a copy.

Route 8:

━━ ━━ ━━ ━━ ━━ ━━ ━━ ━━ ━━ ━━ ━━ ⮕

Georgian Bay Islands National Park

This is another somewhat busier, but more sheltered Georgian Bay trip like The Massasauga (Rte. 7). Also like the previous route, park land is mixed with private land, and there is a fair amount of boat traffic—if you want to paddle this area in the summer, you would be well advised to avoid weekends in general, but especially the long ones. Motorboat traffic and use of the park in general drops off sharply after Thanksgiving. This may be the best time to paddle the island: During the colder fall nights, the wood stoves and picnic shelters come into their own.

TRIP HIGHLIGHTS: Good scenery, very sheltered paddle.

TRIP RATING:

> *Beginner/Intermediate:* 16-mile circumnavigation of Beausoleil Island or six-mile round-trip from Honey Harbour to Honeymoon Bay and back.

TRIP DURATION: One to two days.

NAVIGATION AIDS: CHS chart 2239; Canadian topographic map: *Penetanguishene* (31 D/13).

CAUTIONS: Motorboat traffic; expect cold water if you paddle in spring or fall (wet suit or dry suit recommended).

TRIP PLANNING: Unlike most of the provincial parks around the bay, Georgian Bay Islands National Park is open year-round. This makes it a good place to try some extended-season paddling; both day trips and overnight paddles are possible (until the water freezes, that is). This is an extremely popular park with motorboaters, and if the drone of engines drives you nuts, you will definitely want to schedule your trip for the off-season (before

Victoria Day or after Labor Day). If you are going to try camping on the island during peak season, try asking for a site without a dock. Another option is to try the primitive campsites on some of the smaller islands nearby, such as Centennial Island or Island 95. Permits are required for camping and can be purchased at the park building next to the launch area at Honey Harbour.

LAUNCH SITE: From Highway 400, take Muskoka Road 5 and go north/west for 7.6 miles to the township landing. There is a public lot (day use only) next to the ramp and docks. On the other side of the library building next to the parking lot is the park office where you may buy permits, pick up a map of Beausoleil Island, and choose your campsites if you are staying overnight. If you are camping on the island, you will need to move your car to another lot: Most convenient is Joe's lot, directly across the road from the park office. Ask at the park office for the location of other parking lots in the area if Joe's is full. You will have to pay for parking no matter where you go in Honey Harbour.

DIRECTIONS

START: From the township landing, paddle northwest and then north toward **Deer Island.** *Caution:* This is a busy channel, and the numerous shoals limit the motorboats to certain areas. Keep an eye out for traffic.

MILE 2.5: Paddle between Deer and **Petite Beausoleil Islands**, then turn and paddle northwest along the shore of **Beausoleil Island.** The northern end of the island is the most appealing visually, with its narrow winding channels of gray rock and scattered beaches. There are two camping areas in the northeastern section, complete with picnic shelters. If you stop at these small beaches, be sure to pull your boats up out of reach of the waves from passing boats. Continue paddling and follow the shore of Beausoleil as it bends westward.

MILE 3.0: Honeymoon Bay is a pretty spot and makes a good break and turn-around trip for those who are doing the day paddle. Return to Honey Harbour by the same route if you are turning back or continue paddling west.

MILES 3.0–5.0: Choose a path through the islands north of Beausoleil, most of which are privately owned. Those few belonging to the park are

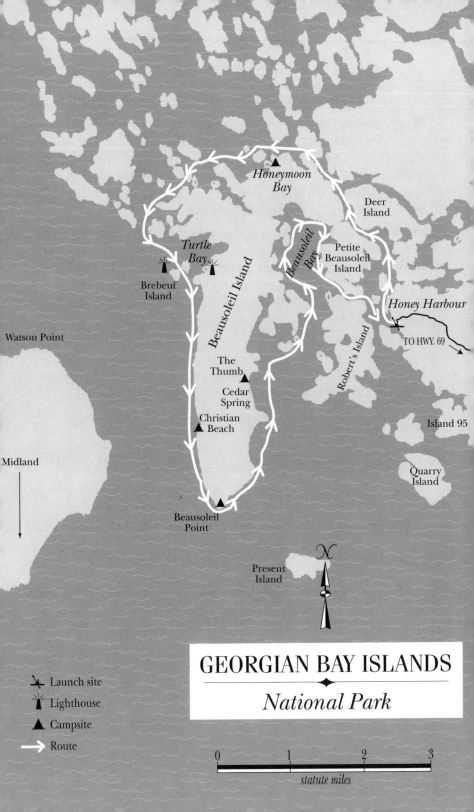

Honeymoon
Bay

Deer
Island

Turtle
Bay

Brebeuf
Island

Beausoleil
Bay

Petite
Beausoleil
Island

Honey Harbour

Watson Point

Beausoleil Island

TO HWY. 69

The
Thumb

Cedar
Spring

Christian
Beach

Robert's Island

Island 95

Midland

Quarry
Island

Beausoleil
Point

N

Present
Island

GEORGIAN BAY ISLANDS
National Park

Launch site

Lighthouse

Campsite

Route

0   1   2   3

statute miles

marked with signs. Several of the bays along the north side of the island have small beaches. Turn and paddle slightly south of west as best you can. Sometimes it is hard to tell the smaller islands from the peninsulas and points of Beausoleil, but keep an eye on your compass and heading.

MILES 5.0–6.0: Paddle around the northwestern tip of the island and turn to the southeast. To the east is **Turtle Bay**, a shallow area with many shoals/islets. The island with the light on it is **Brebeuf Island** (Mile 6.0), which is owned by the Coast Guard and not part of the park. Directly opposite Brebeuf on Beausoleil is another light on a metal tower. Paddle south along the shore of Beausoleil Island.

MILES 6.0–8.0: *Caution:* From Brebeuf Island to the southern tip of Beausoleil is the section of this trip most exposed to wind and waves. Use caution in strong to moderate westerlies/northwesterlies. The shoreline is not good for landing a kayak in any kind of surf (the beaches have lots of rocks and boulders), and it is shallow some distance off shore, which can cause any waves present to get higher and steeper.

MILE 8.0: There is a small sand beach at the **Christian Beach** group campsite (which is available to kayak groups), but beware of a few boulders in the water if you are landing there. Otherwise, continue south toward Beausoleil Point.

MILE 9.5: **Beausoleil Point** has another campground (but no dock), but the point itself is not great to land on—try the beach just west of the point. Turn and begin paddling north along the island's eastern shore.

MILES 9.5–11.0: The east side of the island is much sandier and consists of sand beaches between rocky points. Once you are on this side of the island, you will be in sheltered waters. The only thing to be aware of is that the bay between Beausoleil and **Roberts Islands** is very shallow, enough so that a strong southerly wind could make it uncomfortably choppy. The **Cedar Spring campground** at Mile 11.0 has a large set of docks and buildings, with group campsites, a visitor center, ranger station, and phone.

MILE 12.0: The next point up (near **"The Thumb"**) has another campground and even showers. Just beyond is **Chimney Bay**, a shallow grassy area. Paddle northeast to get around the next point.

MILES 13.0–15.0: Now you are in **Beausoleil Bay**, a pleasant area. Look for a picnic area on the east side of the bay. Follow the shore as it arcs around to the south again, then paddle down the west side of Petite Beausoleil to the **passage** between Petite Beausoleil and Roberts Islands that leads back to Honey Harbour.

MILES 15.0–16.0: Paddle southeast to reach Honey Harbour and the township landing once again.

Where to Eat & Where to Stay

RESTAURANTS & LODGING There are a number of inns and resorts in Honey Harbour and surrounding towns. The park has put together a list for visitors to the area. The **Inn at Christie's Mill** in Port Severn seems to be a favorite, although it was closed for remodeling when we were there; call (705) 538–2354 for information. For a copy of the park's list of local hotels and resorts, call (705) 756–2415. **CAMPING** The **Bluewater Resort** in Honey Harbour has a small campground. Call (705) 756–2454 for more information. The nearest provincial park is **Six Mile Lake**, which is inland from Honey Harbour. Call (705) 756–2746 for information.

Route 9:

━━ ━━ ━ ━ ━ ━━ ━━ ━ ━ ━ ━━ ━━ ━ ➡

Bruce Peninsula: Hope Bay to Lions Head

The Bruce Peninsula, a narrow finger of land about 50 miles long, separates Georgian Bay from the rest of Lake Huron. The Niagara Escarpment, a line of high dolomite cliffs, follows the eastern shore of the peninsula and ends north of the tip of the peninsula in the islands just offshore. Much of the coast between Hope Bay and Lions Head is privately owned, but the high cliffs and boulder jumble shoreline has kept much of Cape Dundas undeveloped. Lions Head, the other large cape, which has high dolomite cliffs, is a Provincial Nature Reserve, which has been left undisturbed. The famous Bruce Trail, which stretches 500 miles from Lake Ontario to the tip of the Bruce Peninsula, also follows this coast. Enjoy the rock and cliff coast, but be very cautious about the weather, as there are only a limited number of safe landing beaches that are acceptable in rough conditions.

TRIP HIGHLIGHTS: Great scenery, hiking along the Bruce Trail, and rugged dolomite cliff shoreline.

TRIP RATING:
Intermediate: 15-mile trip one way from Hope Bay to Lions Head.

TRIP DURATION: Day trip.

NAVIGATION AIDS: CHS chart 2282, Canadian topographic maps 41 A/14 and 41 A/3 at 1:50,000.

CAUTIONS: Clapotis from cliff and boulder shores, cold water, strong winds funneling off the escarpment walls, rocky coast with few rough-water landing beaches.

TRIP PLANNING: This is a relatively long day trip, so start early to have plenty of time to finish in daylight. Wind speed usually increases in the afternoon; an early start also will improve your chances of avoiding high winds. The water can be very cold with late summer/fall temperatures normally peaking in the 50s, so a wet suit or dry suit is strongly recommended. Always check the marine forecast before setting out (in addition to the usual VHF weather bands, the National Park broadcasts forecasts on FM 90.7)—Georgian Bay is notorious for its fickle and violent weather. Be conservative and paddle only in good weather because there are only a few safe places to land along this rugged shoreline in rough conditions. Shoals and boulders are common along the shore, so be very careful when paddling within a quarter mile of the shore.

LAUNCH SITES:

Hope Bay: Heading north on Highway 9, turn right at the sign for Hope Bay (Beech Street). Follow the road until you come to a small parking lot with bathrooms on the right; the public access beach will be on your left. It is about a 150-foot carry from the parking lot to the sand beach, and there is also a wooden dock at the landing.

Lions Head: From Highway 9 in the town of Lions Head, follow the Tour Boat and Marina signs. There is a $4.00 fee to use the boat ramp.

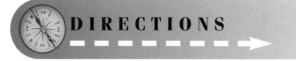

DIRECTIONS

START: From the **public access beach (N 44° 54.16', W 081° 09.37')**, head northeast to follow the south shore of **Cape Dundas**.

MILE 2.5: Heading northeast from the put in, you pass cottages along a shore of large cobbles and small boulders. Just a short distance inland is a bright white dolomite escarpment with cliffs 100 to 150 feet high. At about Mile 2.5 you reach **Jackson Cove**, a lovely little cove that is lined with cottages.

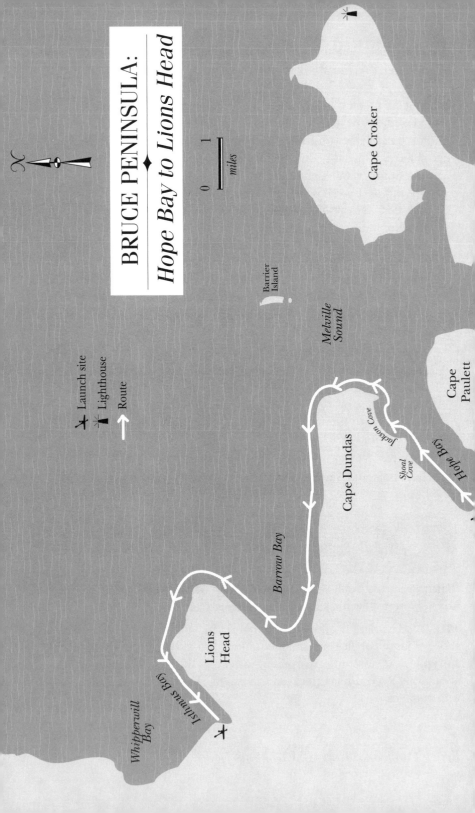

BRUCE PENINSULA:
Hope Bay to Lions Head

Launch site
Lighthouse
Route

0   1
miles

Cape Croker

Barrier Island

Melville Sound

Cape Paulett

Cape Dundas

Jackson Cove

Shoal Cove

Hope Bay

Barrow Bay

Lions Head

Isthmus Bay

Whipperwill Bay

MILE 4.0: At the cove the escarpment ends and the shore is replaced by a low wooded point, rimmed by flat boulders and flat cobblestone beaches. As you approach the tip of Cape Dundas, the slabs of rock become larger, and there are cliffs 20 to 30 feet high along the shore. At the end of the cape, the cliffs become higher—huge flat slabs of rock stand on end or pile up in huge formations along the water's edge.

MILE 6.0: From the tip of the cape, turn west and follow the shore into **Barrow Bay**. The cliffs and flat slabs of fallen rock continue for another 2.0 miles until you reach a cobble and small boulder beach in a small bay with cottages.

MILE 9.0: After the bay with cottages, the wild undeveloped shore returns as do the white dolomite cliffs of the escarpment, rising 100 to 150 feet high at the edge of the shore. At Mile 9.0 you reach the end of Barrow Bay. Here there is a long beach with large cobbles and small boulders. There are cottages along the beach and a stream enters the bay here (**river mouth: N 44° 57.66', W 081° 12.91'**). You can follow the stream inland to a small lake lined with cottages. There does not appear to be any public access to this inland lake.

MILE 10.0: At approximately Mile 10.0, you reach the end of the gravel beach at the end of Barrow Bay. Turn northeast to follow the shore of Lions Head. **Lions Head** is a provincial nature reserve; here the wild

Bruce Peninsula: Hope Bay to Lions Head

undeveloped shoreline begins. As the cottages disappear the high, white dolomite cliffs of the Niagara Escarpment return, rising up from the edge of the water.

MILE 12.0: For 2.0 miles you follow a very rugged coast, with huge boulders lining much of the shore. This would not be a good place to land in rough weather. The white dolomite cliffs continue to follow the shore near the water's edge. At Mile 12.0 you turn the corner and head northwest to round the end of Lions Head.

MILE 13.0: At the end of Lions Head, the shore curves in slightly to form a bay, having a large cobble and boulder beach. In calm conditions this is a suitable place to land. If waves are significant you should stand well offshore because shallow water and boulders extend a considerable distance out.

MILE 15.0: Rounding the corner at the tip of Lions Head, you enter Isthmus Bay and turn southwest and follow the shore to the boat ramp at the town of Lions Head. The northwest coast of Lions Head is similar to the southeast side, with boulder beaches and high, white dolomite cliffs that follow the edge of the shore. Cross the small bay to the take-out point at the **Lions Head Boat Ramp (N 44° 59.46', W 081° 15.0')**.

Where to Eat & Where to Stay

RESTAURANTS Lions Head is a very small town so restaurant choices are limited. For a better selection you will need to drive 25 miles north to the town of Tobermory. For more information on restaurants, call the Tobermory Chamber of Commerce at (519) 596–2452. **LODGING** For lodging you will find the majority of motels near Tobermory. For information call the Tobermory Chamber of Commerce at (519) 596–2452. **CAMPING** There is a city campground near the boat ramp in Lions Head. There is also a small private campground next to the public access point at Hope Bay. Although these campsites are convenient, if you want more rustic undeveloped campsites, you probably should head north toward Tobermory to camp within the **Bruce Peninsula National Park** (519–596–2233).

Route 10:

▬ ▬ ▬ ▬ ▬ ▬ ▬ ▬ ▬ ▬ ▬ ▬ ▬ ▬ ▬ ▬ ▬ ➤

Bruce Peninsula National Park: Tobermory to the Grotto

The Bruce Peninsula, a narrow finger of land about 50 miles long, separates Georgian Bay from the rest of Lake Huron. The Niagara Escarpment, a line of high dolomite cliffs, follows the eastern shore of the peninsula and ends north of the tip of the peninsula in the islands just offshore. At the tip of the peninsula is Bruce Peninsula National Park. Although there are still large private land holdings on the north shore of the Bruce Peninsula, the park contains much of the shore from Tobermory to Cabot Head. The famous Bruce Trail, which stretches 500 miles from Lake Ontario to the tip of the peninsula, follows this coast along the north shore. The northern tip of the Bruce Peninsula has some of the most spectacular shoreline, with the high, white dolomite cliffs of the Niagara Escarpment rising up from the water's edge. At the Grotto and Cave Point, there are sea caves and sculpted cliffs to explore. Enjoy the rock and cliff coast, but be very cautious about the weather because there are only a limited number of safe landing beaches that are acceptable in rough conditions.

TRIP HIGHLIGHTS: Great scenery, hiking along the Bruce Trail, white dolomite cliff shoreline, sea caves (the Grotto).

TRIP RATING:
Advanced: 19-mile round-trip from Tobermory to the Grotto and back.

TRIP DURATION: Long day trip, possible overnight.

NAVIGATION AIDS: CHS chart 2235, Canadian topographic map 41 H/5 at 1:50,000.

CAUTIONS: Clapotis from cliff and boulder shores, cold water, rocky coast with few rough-water landing beaches.

TRIP PLANNING: This is a relatively long day trip so start early to have plenty of time to finish in daylight. Wind speed usually increases in the afternoon; an early start also will improve your chances of avoiding high winds. The water can be very cold with late summer/fall temperatures normally peaking in the 50s. We strongly recommend a wet suit or dry suit. Always check the marine forecast before setting out (in addition to the usual VHF weather bands, the National Park broadcasts forecasts on FM 90.7)— Georgian Bay is notorious for its fickle and violent weather. Strong winds from any northerly direction are sure to bring large seas to this exposed coast. Be conservative and paddle only in good weather because there are only a few safe places to land along this rugged shoreline in rough conditions. Shoals and boulders are common along the shore so be very careful when paddling within a quarter mile of the shore.

LAUNCH SITES:

Big Tub Harbour: Head north on Highway 6 to the end of the peninsula and the town of Tobermory. In Tobermory turn left on Big Tub Road and follow it 1.4 miles to Lighthouse Point Park. There is a small lighthouse, which was established in 1885, at the end of the point. There is an outhouse but no potable water. The flat rock shelf about 100 feet from parking can be used to launch kayaks.

Halfway Log Dump (marginal at best!): This site is an emergency take-out point for road access. It is a 3,250-foot carry, and most kayakers I know would rather paddle the return 9.0 miles than carry a boat over 0.5 mile uphill. From Tobermory head south on Highway 6 and turn off at the Emitt Lake Park access sign. Follow the road 4.9 miles to the trailhead. The trail is an old road that is easy walking, but it is over 0.5 mile to a steep boulder and cobble beach.

DIRECTIONS

START: From the rock shelf at the tip of lighthouse point at the entrance to **Big Tub Harbour (N 45° 15.50', W 081° 40.36')**, head east across the entrance to Little Tub Harbour.

MILE 2.0: Heading east across the bay, you pass **North Point** and paddle along a shoreline of huge boulders and low cliffs. There are some houses along the cliff tops, but there is no safe place to land in rough weather. At Mile 2.0 you round **Dunks Point** and head south into **Dunks Bay**. *Caution:* Watch for submerged boulders off Dunks Point.

MILE 3.0: In a second small bay within Dunks Bay, there is a nice little harbor with a **sand beach (N 45° 15.14', W 081° 38.64')** that provides shelter and a safe landing area even in a strong north wind. All of this shore is private property, so please respect the property holders' rights and only use this landing in an emergency.

MILE 5.0: Leaving Dunks Bay you round a point heading east to reach **Little Cove.** Much of the land between Dunks Bay and Overhanging Point is private—only land in an emergency.

MILE 7.0: Leaving Little Cove you follow the cliff and boulder coast east

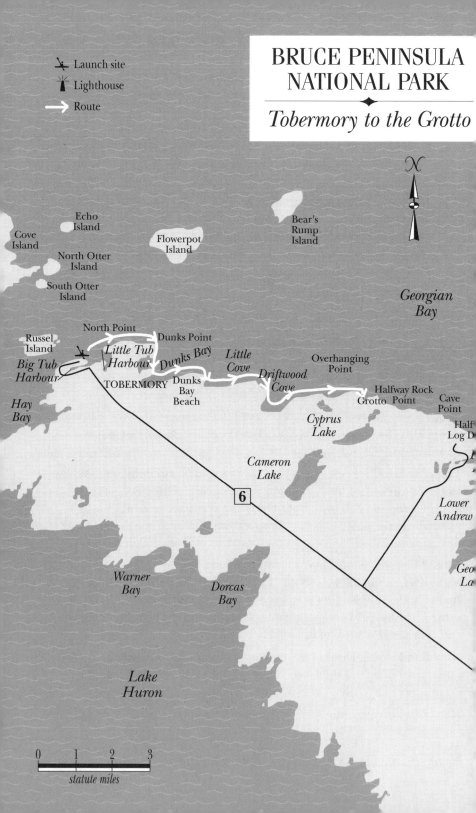

to **Driftwood Cove**. There is some shelter in the cove, and it might be possible to use the steep cobble beach to land in an emergency. There are private land holdings in the cove so only use this beach in an emergency.

MILE 8.5: About 1.5 mile past Driftwood Cove, the shoreline curves in slightly to form a small bay. Here there is another steep cobble beach that could probably be used to land in an emergency. Again, this is still private land.

MILE 9.5: From the small cobble beach the shore again is one of cliffs and huge boulders. As you approach **Overhanging Point**, the high, white dolomite cliffs of the Niagara Escarpment rise directly up from the water's edge. At Mile 9.5 you come to the **Grotto (N 45° 14.71', W 081° 31.46')**. The Grotto is a large sea cave that you normally cannot paddle into because of the shallow rocks and boulders blocking the entrance. Don't be surprised if you see SCUBA (self-contained underwater breathing apparatus) divers pop up inside the Grotto—it has an underwater cave entrance. Just past the Grotto is a second smaller sea cave open to the water. On either side of the Grotto, there are marginal boulder beaches that you can land on in relatively calm seas. (I use the term *beach* here to mean a pile of angular rocks the size of concrete cinder blocks—don't land here if you are averse to scratching your kayak!) From here you can retrace your course to return the 9.5 miles to Lighthouse Point.

Where to Eat & Where to Stay

RESTAURANTS & LODGING For more information on restaurants and motels call the Tobermory Chamber of Commerce at (519) 596–2452. **CAMPING** It may be possible to camp along the route at one of the campsites designated for hikers on the Bruce Trail. However these sites are in high demand, and because they are designed for hikers, not kayakers, you may not be able to find one that is close to the water and a safe shore to land your kayak. For this reason we have recommended that this route be paddled as a day trip out and back. There are many campsites that can be accessed by car at the Cyprus Lake campground. For information on camping within the **Bruce Peninsula National Park** (519) 596–2233.

Route 11:

Fathom Five National Marine Park: Flowerpot Island & Cove Island

The Fathom Five National Marine Park protects over twenty historical shipwrecks and unique geological formations, including sea stacks and sea caves. It is located just offshore of the tip of the Bruce Peninsula. Flowerpot Island is probably the most popular destination among these islands. The island is named for its unique flowerpot-shaped sea stacks, one 23 feet high and a second 39 feet high. Flowerpot Island also has campsites, hiking trails, and a small harbor, making it a very popular destination for nonkayakers as well. In summer boats ferry passengers out to the island several times a day. Cove Island is a much larger island that is less developed and less frequently visited. No camping is allowed, but it is well worth a day visit. At the north end is a beautiful stone-block lighthouse with a tower 80 feet tall. It was built in 1850, but following a delay in receiving the Fresnel lens from France, it was not put into service until 1858. The east side of Cove Island has a beautiful rugged rock and cliff shore very similar to the Canadian north shore of Lake Superior.

TRIP HIGHLIGHTS: Great scenery with a variety of shorelines, including white dolomite cliffs, dark lichen-covered cliffs or huge boulders, an ancient inland sea cave, flowerpots, hiking trails, a beautiful historic lighthouse.

TRIP RATING:

> *Intermediate:* 11-mile loop from Big Tub Harbour around Flowerpot Island and back.
>
> *Advanced:* 20-mile loop from Big Tub Harbour around Flowerpot Island, down the east side of Cove Island, and back to Big Tub Harbour.

TRIP DURATION: Day trip, possible overnight.

NAVIGATION AIDS: CHS chart 2235, Canadian topographic map 41 H/5 at 1:50,000.

CAUTIONS: Clapotis from cliff and boulder shores, cold water, rocky coast with few rough-water landing beaches.

TRIP PLANNING: The advanced paddler's 20-mile route is a relatively long day trip, so start early to have plenty of time to finish in daylight. Even if you do not intend to camp, always bring camping gear and food so that you can stay overnight if the weather does not allow you to return from the islands in one day. Wind speed usually increases in the afternoon—an early start will also improve your chances of avoiding high winds. The water can be very cold with late summer/fall temperatures normally peaking in the 50s. We strongly recommend a wet suit or dry suit. Always check the marine forecast before setting out (in addition to the usual VHF weather bands the National Park broadcasts forecasts on FM 90.7)—Georgian Bay is notorious for its fickle and violent weather. Strong winds from any northerly direction are sure to bring large seas to the islands.

LAUNCH SITE: Head north on Highway 6 to the end of the peninsula and the town of Tobermory. In Tobermory turn left on Big Tub Road and follow it 1.4 miles to Lighthouse Point Park. This small lighthouse at the end of the point was established in 1885. There is an outhouse but no potable water. Use the flat rock shelf about 100 feet from parking to launch kayaks.

DIRECTIONS

START: From the rock shelf at the tip of lighthouse point at the entrance to **Big Tub Harbour (N 45° 15.50', W 081° 40.36')**, head east across the entrance to Little Tub Harbour.

Fathom Five National Marine Park

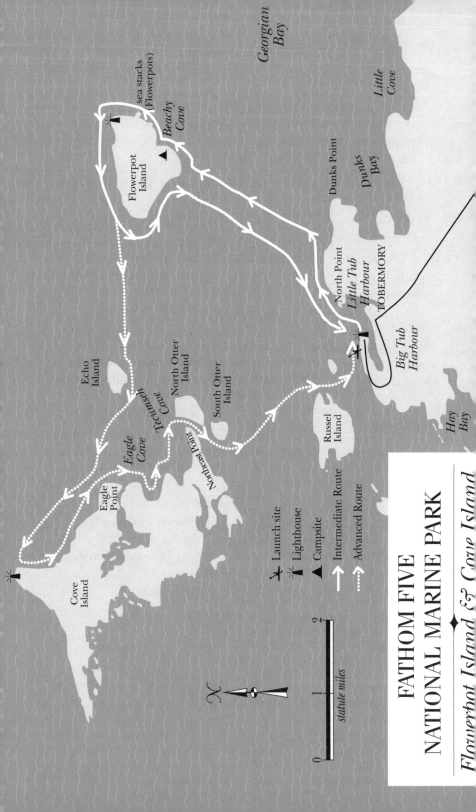

Georgian Bay

Little Cove

sea stacks (Flowerpots)

Beachy Cove

Flowerpot Island

Dunks Point

Dunks Bay

North Point
Little Tub Harbour
TOBERMORY

Echo Island

Big Tub Harbour

North Otter Island

Tecumseh Cove

South Otter Island

Eagle Cove

Eagle Point

Northeast Point

Russel Island

Hay Bay

Cove Island

⊀ Launch site
☀ Lighthouse
▲ Campsite
⟶ Intermediate Route
⋯⟶ Advanced Route

**FATHOM FIVE
NATIONAL MARINE PARK**

Flowerpot Island & Cove Island

statute miles
0   1   2

MILE 1.5: Heading east across the bay, pass North Point and paddle along a shoreline of huge boulders and low cliffs. There are some houses along the cliff tops, but there is no safe place to land in rough weather. At Mile 1.5 you turn north and head for **Flowerpot Island**. The crossing from near Dunks Point is about 2.5 miles.

MILE 4.5: After reaching the island turn east and follow the shore to **Beachy Cove**. There is a small limestone breakwall and two docks—one dock for the six designated campsites and a larger dock for the tour boats **(Beachy Cove Dock N 45° 17.96', W 081° 36.98')**. From the cove there are hiking trails to the Flowerpot, sea stacks which are about 0.3 mile northeast of the dock. Just north of the Large Flowerpot is a trail that leads inland to a large sea cave **(N 45° 18.36', W 081° 36.81')** that was formed about 10,000 years ago when the lake levels were much higher than today.

MILE 5.25: Heading north up the east side of the island, you pass flat rock shelves where you could land a kayak in calm conditions. After about a 0.3 mile, you pass the **Small Flowerpot (N 45° 18.09', W 081° 36.72')**, which rises up 23 feet from the rock shelf on shore. Just down the coast is the **Large Flowerpot (N 45° 18.18', W 081° 36.69')**, a sea stack 39 feet high. Continuing north to Mile 5.25, you come to the **lighthouse**. The original historic lighthouse was a low tower built into the second story of a house. The old lighthouse is gone, and it has been replaced with that basic ugly modern "light on a stick" construction.

MILE 6.0: Near the lighthouse you pass a cliff wall; turn and head west along the north end of the island. At approximately Mile 6.0 paddlers who want to follow the advanced route can continue west and cross toward **Echo Island**. Intermediate paddlers can continue on around Flowerpot then turn south to cross to the mainland and retrace the path to Big Tub Harbour.

MILE 9.0: After a 2.0 mile crossing to Echo Island, a small island with a shore of cliffs and huge boulders. There is no safe beach here for rough-weather landing. Rounding the south end of the island, head to the northwest to the north tip of **Cove Island**.

MILE 13.0: After reaching the north end of Cove Island, you can land on the boulder beach by the boathouse on the northeast tip or on the north tip in front of the lighthouse. Neither beach is suitable for landing in rough weather. The lighthouse **(N 45° 19.61', W 081° 44.12')** is a large white stone-block structure with a tower 80 feet high. The light was put into service in 1858, making it one of the oldest lighthouses on the Great Lakes.

MILE 15.0: Heading southeast down the east side of Cove Island for the first 1.0 mile, you paddle along small boulder and large cobble beaches. Then as you approach **Eagle Point**, the shore changes to huge boulders and low cliffs. At Eagle Point the dark pock-marked limestone has a very different appearance from the white dolomite cliffs of the Niagara Escarpment.

MILE 16.0: Rounding Eagle Point you enter **Eagle Cove**, a lovely rocky cove with a few cobble beaches or flat rock shelves where you could land a kayak. Most of the shoreline continues to be huge boulders or cliffs of dark limestone.

MILE 16.5: Rounding a second point you enter **Tecumseh Cove**. Watch for the orange buoys that mark the wreck of the *Charles C. Minch*, a 154-foot-long schooner that was driven onto the rocks in 1882. The wreck is broken in many pieces and lies in from 20 to 50 feet of water. Water clarity is excellent, and on a glass calm day, you may be able to see parts of the wreck.

MILE 17.0: Leaving Tecumseh Cove you round **Northeast Point**, heading south between the point and North and South Otter Islands.

MILE 20.0: From Northeast Point and the **Otter Islands**, you continue south, passing the east side of **Russel Island** to return to Lighthouse Point at Big Tub Harbour.

Where to Eat & Where to Stay

RESTAURANTS & LODGING For more information on restaurants and area motels, call the Tobermory Chamber of Commerce at (519) 596–2452. **CAMPING** It may be possible to camp at one of the six campsites on Flowerpot Island. These campsites often fill up with campers who come out on the tour boats. Reservations may be allowed in 1999 and after, check with the **Fathom Five National Marine Park** to see if it is possible to reserve a site (519–596–2503). On the mainland there are many campsites that can be accessed by car at the Cyprus Lake campground. For information about camping within the **Bruce Peninsula National Park**, call (519) 596–2233.

Route 12:

━━ ━━ ━━ ━━ ━━ ━━ ━━ ━━ ━━ ━━ ━━ ━━ ━━ ━━ ➤

Pinery Provincial Park

Pinery Provincial Park is known for its coastal dunes, which began forming about 6,000 years ago on the shores of what was then Lake Nipissing. As the water levels retreated, a dry sandy forest called Oak Savanna was established. Oak Savanna is recognized as a globally threatened habitat, which supports many rare plant and animal species. Inland from the dunes is a Carolinian forest and an old river channel that once carried the main flow of the Ausable River before it was diverted to its current riverbed. The marshy shores of the old river channel are an excellent place for bird watching and for viewing other wildlife. Following the old river channel to the river mouth at Port Frank, you get a mix of inland marsh paddling and Lake Huron beach and sand dune shoreline.

TRIP HIGHLIGHTS: Bird watching, coastal sand dunes, unique forest habitat (Oak Savanna and Carolinian forests).

TRIP RATING:
Beginner/Intermediate: About 9 miles one way from the dam on the old river channel to Picnic Area 1.

TRIP DURATION: Day trip.

NAVIGATION AIDS: CHS chart 2260, NOAA chart 14862, Canadian topographic map 40 P/5 at 1:50,000.

CAUTIONS: Shallow water extends far offshore, large breaking waves along the route with winds from the north.

TRIP PLANNING: Check the marine forecast and look at the wave and surf conditions at Picnic Area 1 before starting your trip. If you don't have a second car for a shuttle, you can use a bicycle (the park has a great paved bike path). Another option is to start at the north bridge (adding about 2.5 miles to the route and a portage over the dam), which then leaves a short hike of about 1.0 mile to return to your car from Picnic Area 1.

LAUNCH SITE: Follow the park signs to the park canoe landing. You can put in at the canoe landing, which has parking close to the water and a sandy beach, but no bathrooms. To avoid a portage over the dam you can alternatively put in on the southwest corner of the dam, where there is parking by the side of the road, or back in the Riverside campsites. Bathrooms and potable water are available in the Riverside campsites.

DIRECTIONS

START: From the **canoe landing (N 43° 15.01', W 081° 50.53')** head to the dam and portage the short distance to continue west down the old river channel. Most paddlers will want to start at the southwest corner of the dam so that they can avoid this portage.

MILE 1.5: After paddling about 1.5 miles down the old river channel, you come to the **Burley Bridge**, which has a culvert running under the road. Depending on water levels and/or activities of busy beavers, you may or may not need to make the short portage over the road.

Pinery Provincial Park

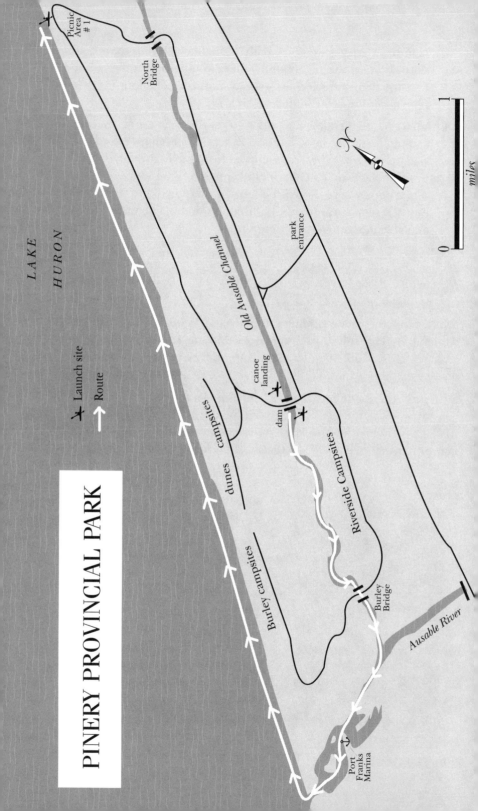

PINERY PROVINCIAL PARK

LAKE

HURON

✈ Launch site
→ Route

Picnic Area # 1

North Bridge

Old Ausable Channel

park entrance

canoe landing

dunes campsites

Burley campsites

Riverside Campsites

dam

Burley Bridge

Ausable River

Port Franks Marina

miles

0   1

MILE 2.0: After the Burley Bridge the old river channel reaches a short narrow section and then goes back to its previous width. After about 0.5 mile from the bridge, the old river channel empties into the **Ausable River**.

MILE 3.0: On reaching the Ausable River, turn right and head west downstream to Lake Huron. At Mile 3.0 you reach the mouth of the river and Port Franks **(River Mouth-Port Franks Marina: N 43° 14.02', W 081° 54.30')**. *Caution:* The river current running against the incoming surf can create very steep breaking waves. Scout the river mouth before continuing to ensure that surf conditions are within your abilities.

MILES 4.0–9.0: From the river mouth head northeast along the coast toward the park. You will pass by several private homes, and at Mile 4.0, almost exactly 1.0 mile from the river mouth, you will reach the park's boundary. When entering the park you pass along beautiful coastal dunes and sand beaches. Enjoy the dunes, but be careful not to damage the fragile dune grass that holds the dunes together. At Mile 9.0 you come to the **parking lot** for Picnic Area 1 **(N 43° 17.20', W 081° 48.19')** and the end of your trip.

Where to Eat & Where to Stay

RESTAURANTS   Just east of the park entrance on Highway 21 is the **Pineview Restaurant**. To the southwest of the park entrance in Port Franks is the **Pinery Inn Restaurant and Motel**. There are more restaurants in the town of Grand Bend to the northeast of the park. For information call Lambton County Tourist information at (800) 265–0316. **LODGING**   For information on motels in the area, call Lambton County Tourist information at (800) 265–0316. **CAMPING**   The Pinery has more than 1,000 designated campsites, so there is no shortage of camping within the park. In spite of the huge number of campsites within the park, campsites are wooded and widely spaced, so you don't feel crowded. For information on camping within the park, call (519) 243–2220.

Lake Huron
Michigan

Route 13:

━━ ━━ ━━ ━━ ━━ ━━ ━━ ━━ ━━ ━━ ━━ ━━ ➤

Port Austin: Point aux Barques

Port Austin is a popular resort area with beautiful sand beaches and Point aux Barques, a sandstone headland that has sea caves and a sea stack. About 1.5 miles off the headland is the Port Austin Shoal Light, an interesting lighthouse on an offshore crib that advanced paddlers may want to add to the route. The route along the coast from Grindstone City passes a variety of shoreline, with cliffs, cobblestone beaches, and sand beach. To the east of Grindstone City—about 3.5 miles on Highway 25—is the Point aux Barques Lighthouse and Museum, which is worth checking out as a sidetrip when running the shuttle to Grindstone City.

TRIP HIGHLIGHTS: Sand beaches, sandstone cliffs, and sea caves.

TRIP RATING:

Intermediate: 7.5-mile trip one way from Grindstone City to Port Austin.

TRIP DURATION: Day trip.

NAVIGATION AIDS: NOAA chart 14863, USGS: *Port Austin East* (7.5 minute).

CAUTIONS: Shoals and boulders far offshore, clapotis off the cliffs and sea caves. Avoid this route if winds are from a northerly direction because the sandstone cliffs and sea caves at Point aux Barques produce clapotis and confused seas. Boulders and shoals extend from shore so use caution when paddling within 1 mile of shore.

TRIP PLANNING: With the exception of a small public access site in Eagle Bay, there is no public access along the shore. Plan to stay in your boat from launch to take out.

LAUNCH SITES:

Port Austin Boat Ramp: Take Highway 25 to Port Austin and watch for the sign for the marina and boat ramp. The boat ramp is just off the highway; it has bathroom facilities and potable water.

Grindstone City Boat Ramp: From Highway 25 head east out of Port Austin for about 8 miles and turn left at the sign for the Grindstone City Boat Ramp (Pearson Road). The boat ramp accesses a small harbor at the mouth of a stream. There is an outhouse, but no potable water at this public access ramp.

DIRECTIONS

START: From the **Grindstone City harbor (N 44° 3.34', W 082° 53.63')** head northwest up the coast toward Port Austin.

MILE 1.5: Heading northwest you pass a mixed shoreline of sand, boulders, cobbles, and even low cliffs. In **Eagle Bay** there is a sand beach with a public access site where you can land. After about 1.5 miles you come to a long point and shoal that extends about 0.5 mile offshore. Swing wide of the point and watch out for boulders and shallow water.

MILE 4.0: After clearing the long bars and shoals, you pass along a stretch of sand beach with private homes. At about Mile 4.0 you come to an old pier; the **sandstone cliffs of Point aux Barques** start just past this point.

MILES 4.25–5.25: There are private homes on top of the cliffs, and there is no public access to allow you to land along this section of shoreline. The sandstone cliffs are weathered and undercut with reentrants and small sea caves. On the northeast tip of Point aux Barques is a thin tip of rock called **Thumbnail Rock** and a sea stack named **Turnip Rock**. *Caution:* Even in moderate seas the cliffs and sea caves can create confused seas and clapotis.

MILES 5.25–7.5: After rounding the point look seaward and see the **Port Austin Reef Light** about 1.5 miles offshore. There is a shoal that extends from shore to the light so watch out for boulders and shallow water; you can easily run aground as far as 1.0 mile offshore. After clearing the shoal, there is a 2.0-mile section of relatively undeveloped sand beach and shallow offshore water. At Mile 7.5 you reach the **Port Austin Boat Ramp (N 44° 2.91', W 082° 59.66')**.

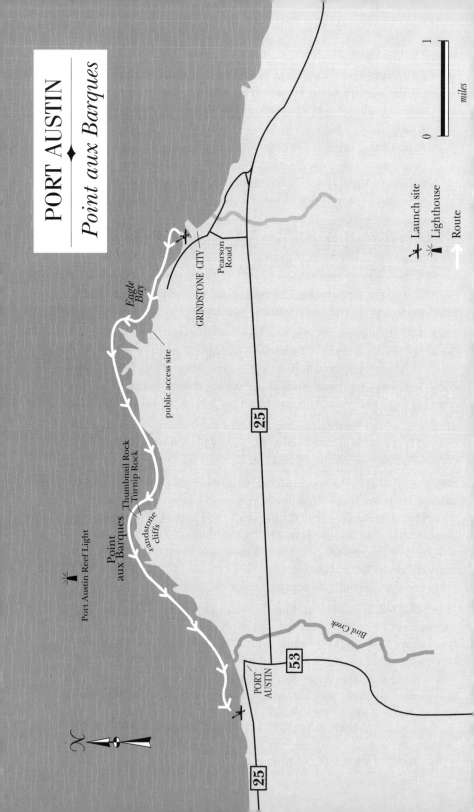

Where to Eat & Where to Stay

RESTAURANTS & LODGING There are several restaurants and motels in the area. Call the Port Austin Chamber of Commerce at (517) 738–7600 for information. **CAMPING** Just east of the Point Aux Barques lighthouse is a county campsite. To the west of Port Austin is Port Crescent State Park. There are also private campgrounds in the area. For information on camping call the Port Austin Chamber of Commerce at (517) 738–7600.

Route 14:

Negwegon State Park

The Negwegon State Park includes 2,400 acres of land and 8 miles of Lake Huron coast. The route from Black River to Ossineke includes the full 8-mile coast of the park with only short sections of private land holdings. The shoreline consists of cobble and sand beaches and many shoal and marsh areas, a perfect habitat for waterfowl and wading birds. Off South Point there are two low islands, Bird Island and Scarecrow Island, which are part of the Michigan Island National Wildlife Refuge. In the summer nesting season, both islands are teeming with bird life, with large gull, heron, and cormorant rookeries. The Thunder Bay area also had great spiritual significance to the early Native Americans of the region. In all ninety-eight small carved stone disks dated to the twelfth century have been found in this region. The disks depict sacred symbols, including *Michi-gi-zhik*, the Great Medicine Tree; *Me-she-pe-shiw*, the horned lynx that raises storms on the lake by thrashing its tail; and *Ah-ne-mi-ke*, the Thunderbird from whom Thunder Bay gets its name. Four of these carved stone disks were found near South Point under the roots of a tree that had been knocked down by high winds. The name *Ossineke* is an Anglicized version of the Algonquian word *Waswsineke*, which means image stones. Within the park near South Point, there are stone-lined pits and long lines of stones that are being studied as possible Native American ruins. If you come across any of these ruins, please respect them and leave the sites undisturbed.

TRIP HIGHLIGHTS: Wild undeveloped coast, great bird watching, Native American ruins.

TRIP RATING:

Beginner/Intermediate: A 9-mile trip one way down the coast from Black River to Ossineke. Beginners should only paddle this trip in calm seas.

Intermediate/Advanced: A 9-mile trip one way down the coast from Black River to Ossineke, plus a sidetrip to Bird and Scarecrow Islands off of South Point. The sidetrip adds a 4-mile round-trip for a total of 13 miles.

TRIP DURATION: Day trip.

NAVIGATION AIDS: NOAA chart 14864; USGS: *Hubbard Lake* (44083-E1) at 1:100,000.

CAUTIONS: Boulder and cobble shore makes it difficult to land in rough conditions; shoals and boulders are common far from shore.

TRIP PLANNING: Always check the marine forecast before heading out. Winds from the north or east can produce large seas. The water is very shallow along the coast, so watch out for shallow boulders offshore and be aware that the main surf break may be up to 1 mile offshore. If you are making the sidetrip to the islands, only do so in calm weather as the shoals surrounding the islands can produce large breaking waves as much as 2 miles offshore.

LAUNCH SITES:

Black River: From Harrisville go north on Highway 23 to Black River Road (about 12 miles north of the intersection of Highways 73 and 23 in Harrisville). Turn right (east) and follow for 2.8 miles to Lakeshore Drive. Turn right on Lakeshore Drive for less than 0.1 mile, and you come to the sign for the boat ramp (just before you cross the river). The DNR public boat ramp is on the Black River, which empties into Lake Huron. The site has outhouse bathroom facilities, but does not have potable water.

Negwegon State Park: From Harrisville go north on Highway 23 to Black River Road (about 12 miles north of the intersection of Highways 73 and 23 in Harrisville). Turn right (east) and follow for about 1.5 miles until you see a small cemetery on the left (north) side of the road—take the next left on Sand Hill Trail Road. Note that Sand Hill Trail Road looks like a poorly graded private sand road and may not have a sign. Follow Sand Hill Trail Road for 2.7 miles, then turn right on to the well-graded gravel road by the state park signs. The gravel road takes you to the water access after 1.2 miles. There is a nice sand beach about 500 feet from the parking lot. Also outhouse bathroom facilities and potable water from an artesian well are available.

Ossineke: From Highway 23 head north (about 7.6 miles north of Black River Road) to the small town of Ossineke, and turn right (east) on Nicholson Hill Road. Follow the road for 2.4 miles to the DNR boat ramp. There is an outhouse, but potable water is not available at the site.

DIRECTIONS

START: From the **Black River boat ramp (N 44° 48.86', W 083° 18.18')** head out into Lake Huron, then turn left to follow the coast north to Negwegon State Park.

MILE 1.0: For the first 0.5 mile the shoreline is sand beach with some small boulders, and the shore is lined with private homes. At Mile 1.0 after the private homes end, the **Negwegon State Park** shore is mostly beautiful sand beach with a few sandbars and rocky points.

MILE 3.0: As you enter the state park, the sand beach shoreline continues with a mixed forest of pine and birch. Negwegon, from the Algonquian language, means "fine plains." At Mile 3.0 you come to a point in the park where there is an artesian well and road access **(N 44° 51.32', W 083° 19.32')**. At approximately Mile 3.25 the sand beach disappears and the shoreline consists of large cobbles and small rounded boulders.

MILE 4.0: At Mile 4.0 there is a nice sand beach about 0.25 miles long that is a safe place to land **(N 44° 52.32', W 083° 19.13')**.

MILE 5.0: From the sand beach the shore quickly returns to large cobbles and small boulders. At Mile 5.0 there is a long rocky point, **South Point (tip of the point: N 44° 52.95', W 083° 18.84')**. There are trails leading to the point from the park. If you follow the trails inland and search just off the trail, you may be able to find some of the Native American ruins (stone-lined pits, lines of stones from old stone walls, etc.). Please leave any artifacts that you find undisturbed.

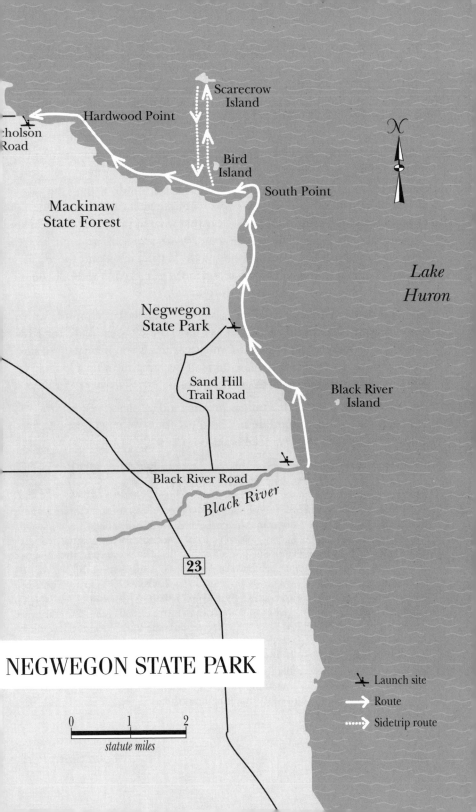

Scarecrow
Island

Hardwood Point

cholson
Road

Bird
Island

South Point

Mackinaw
State Forest

Lake
Huron

Negwegon
State Park

Sand Hill
Trail Road

Black River
Island

Black River Road

Black River

23

NEGWEGON STATE PARK

Launch site

→ Route

Sidetrip route

0   1   2

statute miles

MILE 6.0: Rounding South Point heading west, you see **Bird Island** about 0.5 mile offshore; beyond that is **Scarecrow Island** about 2.0 miles offshore. Intermediate or advanced paddlers may want to make a sidetrip to the islands—4.0 miles round-trip. *Caution:* There are shoals and shallow boulders between South Point and Scarecrow Island, and breaking waves on the shoals are likely even 2 miles offshore, so only make this sidetrip when you have calm seas. Both islands are teeming with bird life, with gull and cormorant rookeries. During nesting season keep a reasonable distance from shore to keep from disturbing the nesting birds. Watch the shallow rocks carefully on a calm day at Scarecrow Island, and you will discover that what at first glance appear to be natural reefs are actually human-made leads and walls for a huge funnel-shaped fish trap. If you choose to follow the mainland shore rather than visit the islands, stay well offshore as there is a wide, shallow area of cobble flats with a marshy shoreline.

MILES 6.0–8.5: The wide, shallow cobble and marsh flats continue with the shoreline edged with reeds and cattails. This is a great place for bird-watchers to view wading birds. At some water levels you may need to stay well offshore, and landing may be difficult because it can be a long slippery walk over the rocks to get to shore.

MILES 8.5–9.0: The last 0.5 mile is private land so please respect the property owners' rights and do not land except in an emergency. At Mile 9.0 you reach the Ossineke boat ramp.

Where to Eat & Where to Stay

RESTAURANTS   When sea kayakers gather in the area for a kayaking event, the **John A. Lau Saloon** in Alpena becomes their unofficial headquarters. This frontier-style saloon has a great selection of beers, and yes, it serves food as well. The small towns of Harrisville and Ossineke do have restaurants, but a better selection is available in the larger town of Alpena. For information call the Alpena Convention and Visitors Bureau (800–425–7362). **LODGING**   There are a few lodging options in Harrisville, but a much better selection is available in Alpena. Call the Alpena Convention and Visitors Bureau (800–425–7362) for more information. **CAMPING**   The **Negwegon State Park** does not have developed campsites at this time. Wilderness camping within the park is allowed without any permit being required by the state park. In theory you are required to get a free permit from the DNR (available at any DNR office) to camp on any state lands. There are also several private campsites in the area. Call the Alpena Convention and Visitors Bureau for more information about them.

Negwegon State Park

The Annual Great Lakes Lighthouse Festival & the Sturgeon Point Lighthouse

Every year, starting the second weekend in October, Alpena hosts the Great Lakes Lighthouse Festival. The event includes booth displays by various nautical gift shops and maritime preservation societies, concerts, lectures, and tours (by land, sea, and air) of over a dozen historical lighthouses in the area. For information about the festival or touring local lighthouses, call Marv or Joy Theut at the Huron Lights Store (517) 595–3600. One lighthouse well worth visiting is the Sturgeon Point Lighthouse, located about 8 miles south of the Black River boat ramp. From the bridge over the Black River head south for 7.4 miles on Lakeshore Drive, then turn left (east) on Point Road for 1.2 miles. The lighthouse began service in 1870, and in 1876, a lifesaving station was also established here. This beautiful and historic lighthouse has a very tall white brick tower and a small museum.

At the end of the point is the long cobble and gravel bar that was given the name of Sturgeon Point because of the huge numbers of sturgeon that would return to the bar to spawn every year. In the 1800s the giant fish (up to 12 feet in length) often damaged nets, and they were not considered a marketable fish. Fishermen would gaff spawning sturgeon off the point by the hundreds, pile them like cordwood on shore, and leave them to rot.

Route 15:

━━ ━ ━━ ━ ━━ ━ ━━ ━ ━━ ━ ━━ ━ ━━ ━ ━━ ━ ━━ ➤

Rockport to Thunder Bay Island

Lake Huron, the second largest of the Great Lakes, has an interesting maritime history, which includes 40 percent of all Great Lakes shipwrecks. The Thunder Bay region was often referred to as the shipwreck coast, with over 160 known shipwrecks in the immediate area. The National Oceanic and Atmospheric Administration (NOAA) has proposed making this area into the Thunder Bay National Marine Sanctuary. The Thunder Bay area also had great spiritual significance to the early Native Americans of the region (see Rte. 14). The coast from Rockport to Thunder Bay Island includes the historic lighthouses on Middle Island and Thunder Bay Island and a shipwreck visible in shallow water along the shore of North Point. You will also find the remains of lifesaving stations on both Middle and Thunder Bay Islands, including an offshore boathouse that still stands on Thunder Bay Island. In spite of its less than inviting name, Misery Bay is a lovely shoal and marsh area ideal for bird-watchers. By entering a long shallow arm of water that leads inland from Misery Bay, you can explore a submerged sinkhole where the water depth plummets from less than 1 foot deep to depths of up to 80 feet in about a kayak length.

TRIP HIGHLIGHTS: Historic lighthouses, great bird watching, and an underwater sinkhole.

TRIP RATING:

Intermediate/Advanced: A 35-to-40-mile round-trip paddle from Rockport to Thunder Bay Island and back.

TRIP DURATION: Overnight or multiday.

NAVIGATION AIDS: NOAA chart 14864; USGS: *Alpena County* at 1:100,000.

CAUTIONS: Boulder and cobble shore makes it difficult to land in rough conditions; shoals and boulders are common far from shore. Strong winds and large seas may be focused at the tip of North Point.

TRIP PLANNING: Always check the marine forecast before heading out. Winds from the north or east can produce large seas. The weather in Thunder Bay should not be taken lightly. In August 1965 sustained winds of 109 miles per hour were measured here 6 miles offshore—the highest sustained winds ever measured on Lake Huron. Much of the shore between Rockport and North Point is privately owned so be prepared to spend several hours in your kayak without landing on shore. The water is very shallow along the coast, so watch out for shallow boulders offshore and be aware that the main surf break may be up to 1 mile offshore. If you are paddling to the islands off North Point, only do so in calm weather as the shoals surrounding the islands can produce large breaking waves. Sugar Island and Thunder Bay Island are part of the Michigan Islands National Wildlife Refuge and are posted no trespassing without permitted access. The U.S. Fish and Wildlife Service controls access to the islands; please call them to get permission to land or camp on the islands. In the past they have been friendly to kayakers, so to keep it that way please call ahead to get information about avoiding sensitive nesting areas and protecting rare plants. Call the Shiwasse Refuge manager at (517) 777–5930.

LAUNCH SITE: Head north from Alpena on Highway 23 for about 8 miles to Rockport Road. Turn right (east) for 3.5 miles until you come to the DNR boat ramp by an old quarry. There are outhouse bathroom facilities, but no potable water.

DIRECTIONS

START: From the **Rockport DNR boat ramp (N 45° 12.14', W 083° 22.90')**, head south along the coast toward North Point.

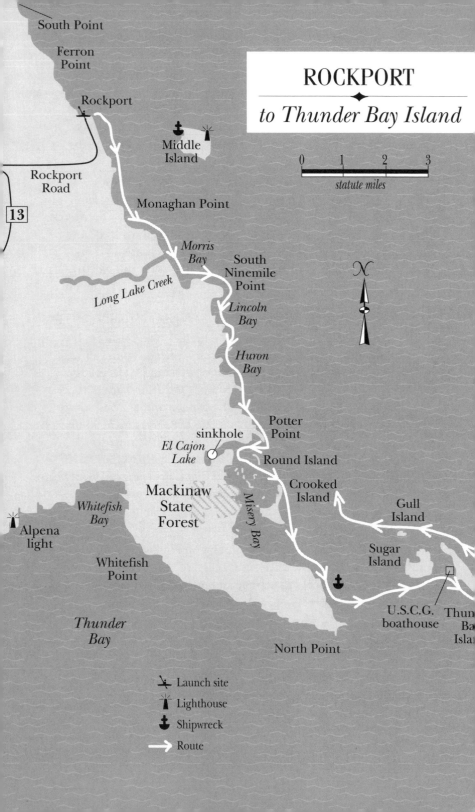

ROCKPORT
◆
to Thunder Bay Island

South Point

Ferron
Point

Rockport

Rockport
Road

13

Middle
Island

Monaghan Point

*Morris
Bay*

South
Ninemile
Point

*Lincoln
Bay*

*Huron
Bay*

Long Lake Creek

0   1   2   3
statute miles

N

sinkhole

*El Cajon
Lake*

Potter
Point

Round Island

Crooked
Island

Gull
Island

Mackinaw
State
Forest

Misery Bay

Sugar
Island

*Whitefish
Bay*

Alpena
light

Whitefish
Point

*Thunder
Bay*

North Point

U.S.C.G.
boathouse

Thun
Ba
Isla

⚓ Launch site
🛆 Lighthouse
⚓ Shipwreck
⟶ Route

MILE 2.5: For the first few miles, you follow a low coast with private homes and cobble beaches. To the east you see Middle Island. (For a description of Middle Island see Rte. 16.) At Mile 2.5 there is a nice sand beach that would be a good place to land in bad weather. The land is probably a private land holding so please only use this beach in an emergency.

MILE 4.0: From the sand beach the shore returns to narrow cobble beaches with private homes until you near **Long Lake Creek** where there is a large sand beach and private homes along the shore.

MILE 6.0: After the sand beach the shoreline returns to narrow cobble beaches with private homes. Paddling past **Morris Bay**, at Mile 6.0 you reach the end of **South Ninemile Point**, where there is flat limestone shelf rock along the shore.

MILE 7.5: After rounding South Ninemile Point, you paddle along **Lincoln Bay** and enter **Huron Bay**. In Lincoln Bay you pass a tiny gravel island with a few trees on it at Mile 7.5. Just past the island is a sand beach with private homes. Then there is a gravel bar point with a steel tower and a navigation light.

MILE 10.0: At Mile 10.0 you round **Potter Point**, a narrow hook-shaped gravel point. Now turn west to enter **Misery Bay**.

MILE 11.0: Heading west into Misery Bay, you need to pick your way over shoals and through very shallow water until you enter a long narrow channel that connects Misery Bay with **El Cajon Lake**. The channel is very shallow and at low lake levels it may not be possible to go through the channel in a kayak. As the channel enters El Cajon Lake, the bottom suddenly drops away from less than 1 foot deep to as deep as 80 feet. The sudden drop-off is due to a **sinkhole** in the limestone bedrock **(N 45° 05.18', W 083° 19.07')**. Springs enter the sinkhole at the bottom, and it is filled with clear, cold water.

MILE 13.0: Paddling back out of the channel into Misery Bay, you head to the southeast and paddle to the outside of **Crooked Island** (also known as Misery Island). The island is privately owned, but on the mainland shore just west of Crooked Island is a section of Mackinaw State Forest where it is possible to land or camp on public land.

MILE 15.5: Heading south from Crooked Island you cross the shallow bay and marsh area to North Point. Heading down the shore you pass a sand beach rimmed by rounded boulders, and you come to a **shipwreck** in shallow water near shore (**N 45° 02.11', W 083° 16.15'**).

MILE 18.5: Weather permitting turn and head east from the shipwreck to make the 2.0-mile crossing to **Sugar Island**. Paddling along the south shore of Sugar Island, continue on to the middle of **Thunder Bay Island**. In the shelter between the islands is a small bay with an offshore boathouse from the old U.S. Coast Guard station. The boathouse was originally connected to Thunder Bay Island by a long dock. Both Sugar Island and Thunder Bay Island are part of the Michigan Islands National Wildlife Area, and they are posted no trespassing without previous authorization. For information on getting permission to land or camp on the islands, call the U.S. Fish and Wildlife Service at (517) 777–5930. Assuming you have permission to land, the cobble beach near the boathouse makes a good sheltered landing because the two islands provide shelter from most wind directions.

MILE 19.5: Heading southeast and rounding the south end of the island, you pass a shoreline of flat slabs of limestone rock. As you round the south end of the island, you may be able to see wreckage of the *Monohansett,* a 167-foot-long ship loaded with coal that burned and sank off the southwest corner of the island in 1907. The wreck now lies in 15 to 20 feet of water. *Caution:* There is a long rock reef that extends far from shore on this southeast corner of the island. You need to paddle well offshore to clear the reef at low lake levels. Just past the reef you see the lighthouse, and in calm weather you could land on the flat limestone slab shore. The lighthouse is one of the oldest lights on the Great Lakes and was first put into service in 1832. In 1857 ten feet of height was added to the tower, making it a total of 50 feet tall; in 1858 a fog bell was added. Thunder Bay Island has an interesting history, in addition to the

lighthouse and Coast Guard station. There was a fishing village of 160 people at a time when the city of Alpena had yet to be founded on the mainland. For more information on the history of the island and to donate your time and money to help preserve the lighthouse and boathouse, contact Captain Burke (517–354–2542) of the Thunder Bay Island Preservation Society.

MILE 21.0: Heading northwest along Thunder Bay Island, you pass flat limestone rock shore, which then becomes cobble and gravel beach. As you round the northwest tip of the island, swing well wide of the point because there is a gravel bar that extends out from the island, and it is easy to run aground here. From the tip of the island, head west to make the 1.0-mile crossing to **Gull Island**.

MILE 22.0: At Mile 22 you reach Gull Island, a small, low gravel island with few trees. This is a gull and cormorant rookery so do not land here during the nesting season, and stay far enough from shore to keep from disturbing the nesting birds. From here it is a 3.0-mile crossing west to Crooked (Misery) Island, and then you can retrace your route north to Rockport for a round-trip distance of 35 to 40 miles.

Where to Eat & Where to Stay

RESTAURANTS When sea kayakers gather in the area for a kayaking event, the **John A. Lau Saloon** in Alpena becomes their unofficial headquarters. This frontier-style saloon has a great selection of beers and yes it serves food as well. The small towns of Harrisville and Ossineke do have restaurants, but a better selection is available in the larger town of Alpena. For information call the Alpena Convention and Visitors Bureau (800) 425–7362. **LODGING** There are a few lodging options in Harrisville, but a much better selection is available in Alpena; call the Alpena Convention and Visitors Bureau (800) 425–7362 for more information. **CAMPING** This trip requires an overnight that can be difficult because most of the land along the route is privately owned or has restricted access. You can camp overnight on the small area of coast that is **Mackinaw State Forest** in Misery Bay set aside for undeveloped wilderness camping. A free DNR permit is required for overnight camping on any state lands (you can pick it up at any DNR office, although many kayakers do not bother with this formality because it is rarely enforced). Both Sugar and Thunder Bay Islands are posted "no unauthorized access" by the U.S. Fish and Wildlife Service. To receive permission to camp on the islands call the **Shiawasse Refuge** manager at (517) 777–5930. For camping on the mainland, there is wilderness camping allowed in **Negwegon State Park** (see Rte. 14), and there are also several private campsites in the area. Call the Alpena Convention and Visitors Bureau at (800) 425–7362 for more information.

Route 16:

----- ----- ----- ----- ----- ----- ----- ----- ----- ----- ----- ----- ----- ----- ----- --->

Middle Island

In the small bay on the northwest corner of the Middle Island is the wreck of the *Portsmith*. The 176-foot ship, loaded with pig iron, ran aground on island shoals in 1867. The wreck of the *Portsmith* is only part of the fascinating history of Middle Island, located about 2 miles off Rockport's shores. In 1881 a lifesaving station was established in the small bay on the northwest end of the island. The lifesaving station was in operation until 1937 and the ruins of the buildings still remain. In 1905 a lighthouse was put into service on the east side of the island. Much of the island is privately owned, so if you want to explore the lighthouse or most of the island, you should get permission from the owners.

TRIP HIGHLIGHTS: Ruins of a lifesaving station, a historic lighthouse, a shipwreck visible in shallow water.

TRIP RATING:
Beginner/Intermediate: A 9-mile round-trip from Rockport to Middle Island, around the island and back.

TRIP DURATION: Day trip.

NAVIGATION AIDS: NOAA chart 14864; USGS: *Middle Island* (7.5 minute).

CAUTIONS: Limestone shelf and cobble shore may make it difficult to land in rough conditions; shoals and boulders are common far from shore. The coast and crossing is unprotected, and large seas can be produced with winds from the north or east. Cold water in spring or fall is also a hazard.

TRIP PLANNING: Always check the marine forecast before heading out. Winds from the north or east can produce large seas. The weather in Thunder Bay should not be taken lightly. In August 1965 sustained winds of 109 miles per hour were measured near Alpena 6 miles offshore—the highest sustained winds ever measured on Lake Huron. In spring or fall the water can be very cold; a dry suit or wet suit is strongly recommended. The northwest corner of the island is public land (see route map), but most of the island is privately owned. Although you can probably land or camp legally on the public lands, you should call the owners of most of the land on Middle Island to let them know that you plan to visit. The owners have had problems with litter and vandalism on the island, but they have been hospitable to kayakers. Please respect their property rights to ensure access for future kayakers. Call Marv or Joy Theut at the Huron Lights (517–595–3600 or at home at 517–595–6722) to ask permission to land on their portion of the island. The Huron Lights Store at 7239 North US 23 also has a small museum with displays on the history of the island.

LAUNCH SITE: Head north from Alpena on Highway 23 for about 8 miles to Rockport Road, then turn right (east) for 3.5 miles until you come to the DNR boat ramp by an old quarry. There are outhouse bathroom facilities, but no potable water.

DIRECTIONS

START: From the Rockport DNR **boat ramp (N 45° 12.14', W 083° 22.90')** head south along the coast.

MILE 1.0: The first 1.0 mile you follow a shoreline of cobble beaches with private homes. To the east you see Middle Island about 2.0 miles offshore. Weather permitting turn east and cross to the bay on the northwest corner of the island.

MILE 3.0: As you enter the bay, watch for the wreck of the *Portsmith*, in the shallows off of Middle Island. Entering the bay you pass over a shoal and into a small but sheltered harbor. There is a privately maintained dock, but you are actually on **Mackinaw State Forest land (N 45°11.81', W 083° 19.99')**. Within sight of the dock are the ruins of the old lifesaving station. Two roads lead to the private lands on the island: one goes east

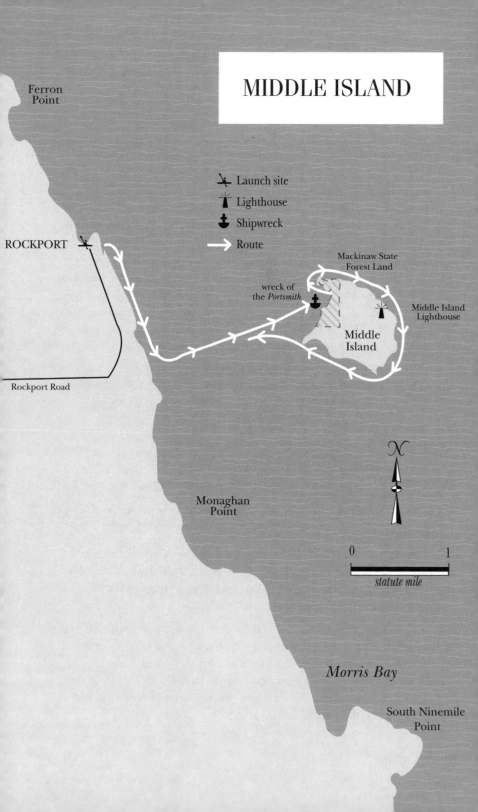

across the island to the lighthouses; a second, which leads south, is a private drive to the Theut's Camp—please do not go down this path even if you have permission to visit the private portion of the island.

MILE 5.0: Heading out of the small harbor and circling the island clockwise, you round a gravel spit and pass along a cobble beach shore. As you paddle along the north and east side of the island, you pass over a shallow limestone shelf. At Mile 5.0, about 2.0 miles from the harbor, you come to the **Middle Island Lighthouse**. The light was put into service in 1905, and several buildings remain, including the old fog signal building and keepers' quarters. Most are in a state of disrepair, but restoration is in progress. This is private land so please do not land here unless you have permission from the Theuts. On a calm day you may be able to land on the limestone shelf or steep cobble beach in front of the lighthouse.

MILE 5.5: Heading south down the east side of the island, you come to a gravel spit.

MILE 6.5: The south side of the island is cobble beach with a very shallow gently sloping bottom. On the west end of the island, there is a long, narrow gravel spit with the remains of an old fishing boat on the top of the gravel bar. From the gravel spit, weather permitting, you can make the return crossing and trip back to Rockport.

Where to Eat & Where to Stay

RESTAURANTS & LODGING   See Route 14: Negwegon State Park. **CAMPING**   The trip is described as a day trip, but it is probably legal to camp on the public lands next to the harbor on Middle Island. Even if you plan to stay on the public land, please let the Theuts know of your plans to visit the island, and get their permission if you want to visit the lighthouse, which is on their land. For camping on the mainland wilderness camping is allowed in Negwegon State Park (see Rte. 14), and there are also several private campsites in the area. Call the Alpena Convention and Visitors Bureau at (800) 425–7362 for more information.

Route 17:

━ ━ ━ ━ ━ ━ ━ ━ ━ ━ ━ ━ ━ ➤

Presque Isle to Thompson Harbor

Presque Isle is a beautiful peninsula with two historic lighthouses. The old lighthouse was built in 1840 near the base of the peninsula, but trees grew tall and began to obstruct the light. The new light was built near the end of the peninsula in 1870. With a tower 113 feet high, it was one of the tallest lights on the Great Lakes. The light was automated in 1970 and is still in operation today. Tours of the lighthouses are available, and there is a museum at the old lighthouse with a $2.00 admission. To the west is Thompson Harbor, an undeveloped coast within the Mackinaw State Forest that includes coastal sand dunes. In an area where much of the coast is privately owned, the state forest land in Thompson Harbor is a welcome oasis of wilderness. There is a short but beautiful stretch of coastal sand dunes and a great sand beach. This is also a great place to find rare wildflowers, including several species of pitcher plants and dwarf lake iris. In the shallow water a short distance offshore, you can view the wreck of the *American Union*, a 500-ton vessel that ran aground in 1894.

TRIP HIGHLIGHTS: Two historic lighthouses, a shipwreck, coastal sand dunes, rare wildflowers.

TRIP RATING:

Beginner/Intermediate: 11-mile round-trip journey from the Presque Isle light to the dunes in Thompson Harbor and back.

Intermediate: 15-mile round-trip journey from the Presque Isle light to the wreck of the *American Union* and back.

TRIP DURATION: Day trip or overnight.

TRIP PLANNING : Always check the marine forecast before heading out. Winds from the north or east can produce large seas (see Rte. 16). In spring or fall the water can be very cold and a dry suit or wet suit is strongly recommended. Overnight camping on state land is possible in Thompson Harbor. To camp on state land a free permit is required by law. Pick one up at any DNR office (in practice few paddlers bother with this formality, and the rule is rarely enforced).

LAUNCH SITES : Head north from Alpena on Highway 23 and watch for the signs to Presque Isle. At the sign for Presque Isle, turn right on County Road 638 and follow it east for 4 miles until you come to Grand Lake Road. Turn left on Grand Lake Road (north), following it for 2 miles until you come to the base of the Presque Isle peninsula. You can launch on the southeast side of the peninsula at the marina in Presque Isle Harbor, but it will add 3 miles to your paddle to Thompson Harbor. For this reason the launch site near the new lighthouse is recommended. Drive out the peninsula to the new lighthouse, then turn left on the road to North Bay. This gravel road dead-ends about 0.25 mile from the lighthouse, where there is a cobble beach on North Bay. Bathrooms and potable water are available at the lighthouse, but not at the cobble beach launch site.

D I R E C T I O N S

START: From the **beach (N 45° 21.28', W 083° 29.68')** head south along the shore of the Presque Isle peninsula.

MILE 1.25: For the first 1.0 mile, you follow the shore of the **Presque Isle** peninsula, with its mixed pine and hardwood forests and narrow cobble beaches. At Mile 1.25 you reach the end of the peninsula and come to privately owned land/homes along the south shore of **North Bay**.

MILE 3.5: Paddle west past the private homes until you reach the start of **Black Point**. At Black Point the wild shore, with mixed forests and cobble beach, returns.

MILE 4.5: At Mile 4.5 you round the end of Black Point. *Caution:* Watch for shallow boulders and shoals off the point. As you round the point, you enter **Thompson Harbor**.

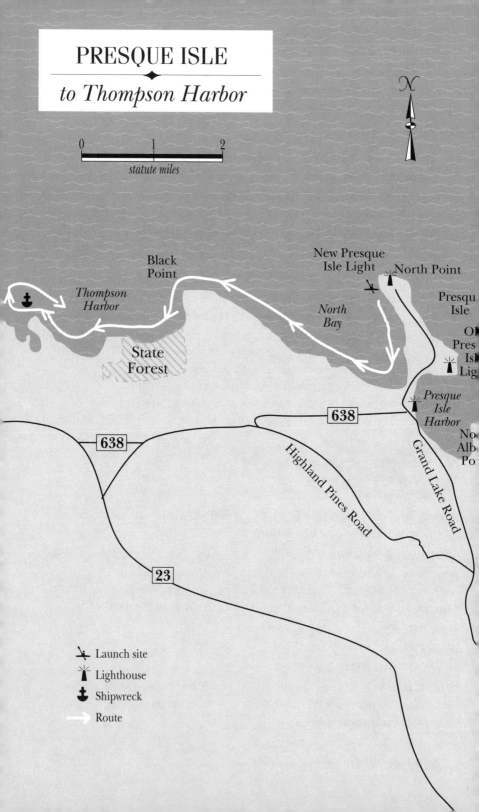

PRESQUE ISLE
to Thompson Harbor

0   1   2
statute miles

N

Black
Point

New Presque
Isle Light

North Point

*Thompson
Harbor*

Presqu
Isle

*North
Bay*

O
Pres
Is
Lig

State
Forest

*Presque
Isle
Harbor*

638

No
Alb
Po

638

Highland Pines Road

Grand Lake Road

23

Launch site

Lighthouse

Shipwreck

Route

MILE 5.5: Entering Thompson Harbor, you come to the first small bay, which has a sand beach and coastal sand dunes (**N 45° 21.07', W 083° 32.96'**). This is a great place for a lunch stop or for overnight camping. The state park land along the coast is only about 1.0 mile long so make sure that you are not on private land (see route map for approximate location of state lands). For the 11-mile Beginner/Intermediate trip, head east from here and retrace your path to the launch site.

MILE 6.5: 1.0 mile farther west you come to a second small bay with a sand beach. This is privately owned land so only use this beach in an emergency.

MILE 7.5: Continuing west you come to two small points. Watch for the wreck of the ***American Union***, a 500-ton vessel that ran aground near Thompson Harbor in 1894. I was unable to find the wreck when I researched the route due to rough conditions, so there is no waypoint given and the position on the route map is approximate. The location of the wreck was described to me as being halfway between Black Point and Observatory Point, about 100 yards from shore in shallow water. As with most shallow wrecks, the wreckage may be scattered over a large area. From the wreck turn east and retrace your steps to the launch site for a 15-mile round-trip.

Where to Eat & Where to Stay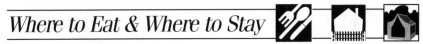

RESTAURANTS, LODGING & CAMPING See Route 14: Negwegon State Park.

Route 18:

━━ ━━ ━━ ━━ ━━ ━━ ━━ ━━ ━━ ━━ ━━ ➤

Mackinac Island & Round Island

Mackinac Island State Park was Michigan's first state park. Today most of the island is protected within the park, giving you 1,780 acres to explore. No motorized vehicles are allowed on the island; it is an ideal area to explore on foot, by bicycle, or in a kayak. This is not a wilderness island by any means. At the south end of the island is a harbor and small city, where ferries bring thousands of tourists to the island every summer. However once you leave the harbor area, you follow a mostly undeveloped shore, where your only company will be cyclists enjoying the road that circles the island. By traveling to the island by kayak, you can enjoy the undeveloped coast and land near the harbor and the historic buildings from the fur-trading era, including Fort Mackinac. High on a hill above the harbor, the view from the famous porch of the historic Grand Hotel (dripping wet kayakers are not welcome inside) is truly grand. The contrast between the quiet undeveloped coastline and the frenzy of the tourist acitivity near the harbor adds to the experience. There is more to Mackinac Island than crowds, gift shops, and fudge! Just across from the harbor is the wild and undeveloped Round Island, which has a historic lighthouse on its northern tip.

TRIP HIGHLIGHTS: A historic lighthouse, Fort Mackinac and other historic buildings from the early fur trade, undeveloped coast on an island where motor vehicles are not allowed.

TRIP RATING:
   Intermediate: 16-mile round-trip journey from Saint Ignace to Mackinac Island, circling the island and back, including a short sidetrip to Round Island.

TRIP DURATION: Day trip.

NAVIGATION AIDS: NOAA chart 14881; USGS: *Cheboygan* (45084-E1) at 1:100,000.

CAUTIONS: Cobble shore and limestone block shoreline may make it difficult to land in rough conditions; shoals and boulders are common far from shore; cold water in spring or fall.

TRIP PLANNING: Always check the marine forecast before heading out. Winds from the east or west can produce large seas. In spring or fall the water can be very cold, and even in summer a dry suit or wet suit is strongly recommended. Do not attempt the 3.75-mile crossing unless you have good weather. Even if you plan to paddle the route as a day trip, it is prudent to bring enough food for several days and enough camping gear to give you the option of staying overnight on Round Island if you have to wait for better weather. You could probably return by ferry, but getting your kayak across could be a hassle.

LAUNCH SITE: If you are a troll (living under the Mackinac Bridge), take Highway 75 north and cross the Mackinac Bridge to the Upper Peninsula—the bridge fare is $1.50. Watch for the sign for Saint Ignace and follow the signs to the ferry docks. There is a public boat ramp with bathrooms and potable water. The launch fee is $2.00.

DIRECTIONS

START: From the **Saint Ignace boat ramp (N 45° 51.99', W 084° 43.20')**, head northeast along the shore of the harbor. On your way to the ferry docks, make sure you check out the museum ship the USCG *Maple*, which is docked near the boat ramp.

MILE 0.5: Work your way carefully past the ferry docks and head for the point at the northeast corner of the harbor. *Caution:* There is a lot of ferry traffic, and some of the ferries travel at very high speeds. It is best

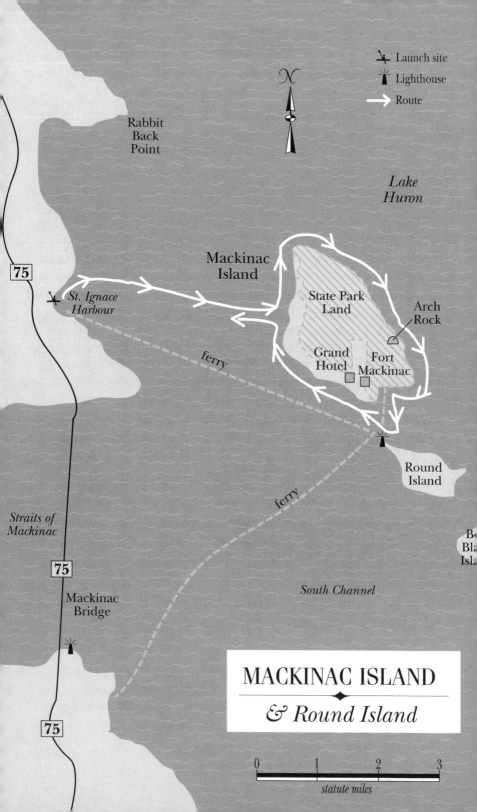

Launch site

Lighthouse

Route

Rabbit
Back
Point

*Lake
Huron*

**Mackinac
Island**

75

St. Ignace
Harbour

State Park
Land

Arch
Rock

ferry

Grand
Hotel

Fort
Mackinac

Round
Island

*Straits of
Mackinac*

75

ferry

B.
Bla
Isl.

South Channel

Mackinac
Bridge

75

MACKINAC ISLAND

& Round Island

0   1   2   3

statute miles

to cross near the docks before they get up to speed, then cross to the island from the point, staying well north of the ferry route (see the route map). From the point head east to make the 3.75-mile crossing to the island.

MILE 4.25: On the west side of the island, you will see a small sheet-piling harbor with a small ferry barge docked in it. From here turn north to circle the island.

MILE 5.25: As you head north along the shore, you pass narrow gravel and cobble beaches and some large blocks of limestone, installed at the edge of the road to control erosion. As you round the north tip of the island, you pass a group of older homes. *Caution:* On the north end of the island, you will pass the remains of an old steel dock in shallow water.

MILE 7.0: As you paddle down the east side of the island, the gravel beach and shoreline with stretches of limestone block for erosion control continues. The paved bike path runs close to the water. As you head south the low shoreline slowly becomes steeper and higher with a few small limestone outcrops. Watch for a small sea cave just inland of the bike path at about Mile 7.0.

MILE 7.5: Watch for **Arch Rock (N 45° 51.48', W 084° 36.34')** a natural arch on a rock outcropping next to shore. There is an observation platform and trails leading to the top of the rock outcropping.

MILE 8.5: At about Mile 8.5 you round the southeast corner of the island and pass by a huge, old resort hotel. Although this is private land, there is a large cobble/small boulder beach where you could land.

MILE 9.0: Continuing you enter the harbor. *Caution:* Watch for ferry traffic entering and leaving the harbor. Look up the hill from the harbor and town, and you will see **Fort Mackinac.** Just south of the harbor is a cobble and boulder beach within the state park where you can land. Although crime is not a big problem on the island, you may want to bring a cable to lock your boat. Get out and explore historical sites; make sure you hike up to enjoy the view from the porch of the **Grand Hotel.**

MILE 9.5: Returning to your kayak, head south to cross to **Round Island.** *Caution:* The channel between the islands can have current. It focuses wave energy between the two islands, producing steep, confused waves with a west or east wind. The harbor's rock breakwaters can produce clapotis, and there is a great deal of ferry traffic. At the north tip of Round Island, there is a long gravel and cobble point with a lighthouse at the end. The Round Island light began service in 1894 and was operated until 1947. In the 1970s high lake levels caused erosion, and the structure was at risk of collapse. State and private donations from historical societies have restored the lighthouse to its original condition. You can land on either side of the point on the steep gravel and cobble beaches **(Round Island Beach by lighthouse: N 45° 50.23', W 084°**

36.92'). Make sure you land on the sheltered side because any surf will dump unmercifully on the shore.

MILE 10.0: As you head north back to Mackinac Island, enjoy the view of the **Mackinac Bridge** to the southwest and the Grand Hotel to the northwest. On reaching the south end of the island, head west to finish your circumnavigation of the island.

MILES 10.0–12.0: Paddling along the southwest side of the island, you pass beautiful old Victorian style houses at the top of a bluff overlooking the lake. As you continue up the west side of the island, the shoreline consists of alternating sections of cobble beach and large blocks of limestone placed to control shoreline erosion. Watch for a street intersection marked by a cannon pointed out over the water (don't worry, it's not loaded). Just north of the cannon is the small sheet-piling harbor and the small ferry barge where you started your trip around the island. From here you can return to the north tip of the Saint Ignace Harbor—weather permitting—making the 3.75-mile crossing.

MILE 16.0: Try to aim for the north end of the harbor to avoid crossing the path of the many ferry boats. Watch the path of the ferries as you cross and adjust your course accordingly. From the point at the north side of the harbor, return to the boat ramp taking care when crossing the ferry docks in the harbor.

Where to Eat & Where to Stay

RESTAURANTS   There are several restaurants within walking distance of the boat ramp in Saint Ignace: **Cassidy's Café, Mackinac Grill,** and **The Galley** (906–643–7960). For other restaurant choices in Saint Ignance call the Saint Ignace Area Chamber of Commerce at (800) 338–6660. **LODGING**   This is a popular tourist destination, and there are several motels available in Saint Ignace. For more information call the Saint Ignace Area Chamber of Commerce at (800) 338–6660. **CAMPING**   The trip is best paddled as a day trip, but it is possible to camp on the public lands on Round Island (part of Hiawatha National Forest) if the weather deteriorates, and it is not safe to cross back to Saint Ignace. For camping in the Saint Ignace area, there is the **Straits State Park**, overlooking the Straits of Mackinac (906–643–8620). There are also several private campgrounds in the area. For information call the Saint Ignace Area Chamber of Commerce.

Route 19:

▬ ▬ ▬ ▬ ▬ ▬ ▬ ▬ ▬ ▬ ▬ ▬ ▬ ▬ ▬ ➤

Les Cheneaux Islands

As part of the limestone arc that includes Manitoulin Island and the Bruce Peninsula, the Cheneaux (Channel) Islands have the white cobblestone beaches typical of the region, very different from the Canadian Shield country just an hour's drive north (see Rte. 1: St. Mary's River). The tightly clustered islands provide shelter from southeasterly winds. Many routes are possible through the islands, but Government Island makes a good place from which to launch day trips, or just to visit for itself. The island is covered with northern white cedar forest and is a pleasant place to camp and walk.

TRIP HIGHLIGHTS: Sheltered island group with many possible day trips and/or good camping on Government Island.

TRIP RATING:
Beginner: 3-mile round-trip from Lakeside Drive boat launch to Government Island and back, with an additional 3-mile circumnavigation of Government Island possible, weather permitting.
Intermediate: Add an 8-mile sidetrip to the beginner trip, from Government Island to Les Cheneaux Channel, a total round-trip distance of 11 miles.

TRIP DURATION: Part day to two days.

NAVIGATION AIDS: NOAA chart 14885, USGS: *Cedarville* at 1:24,000. There is a map of the islands for fishermen, but it also has depths marked on it and is useful for paddlers. Maps are available for a few dollars at the outfitter in Cedarville (see Appendix B).

CAUTIONS: Boat traffic, exposure to southeasterly winds around the outside (southern end) of the island group.

TRIP PLANNING: With so little exposure to wind and waves off the open lake, this makes a good trip almost any time the water isn't "hard," but if you go early in the season be sure to wear a wet suit or dry suit. Use caution, however, when planning to paddle the southern end of the island group. With a fetch of more than 150 miles to the southeast and the extensive shoals around the islands, this is an uncomfortable and even dangerous place to be in rough weather. If the weather deteriorates, better to stay on the inside of the island group. Camping on Government Island is free; no permits are required, and campsites are available on a first-come first-served basis. If an established site is taken, you may have to do without such amenities as a picnic table and trashcan, but the relatively open woods provide extra room for tents if necessary.

LAUNCH SITES: The Lakeshore Drive boat launch is only 1.5 miles from Government Island. From the intersection of Highways M 134 and M 129, drive east on M 134 for 3.0 miles. Turn south onto Lakeshore Drive (marked by a small green street sign), then follow the road through several twists and turns until it does a U-turn and ends at the boat launch. This ramp is mainly used by those going out to island cottages, but there are no parking or launching fees. There is also boat ramp in downtown Cedarville, but it can be quite busy in the summer, and there is no overnight parking. It may be useful, however, if the channel by the Lakeshore Drive launch is uncomfortably choppy. From the intersection of M 134 and M 129 in Cedarville, drive 0.3 mile south on M 129 to the boat ramp on the east side of the road. There is a $2.00 launch fee but no fee for parking.

DIRECTIONS

START: Paddle west past the southern end of **Hill Island** and toward the northwest tip of **Coryell Island**.

MILE 0.5: Once you round the tip of Coryell Island, paddle to the southeast tip of **Island No. 8**.

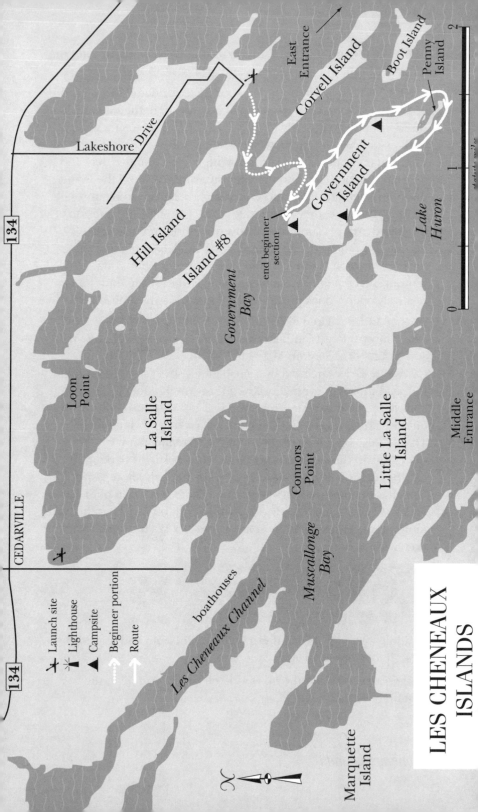

MILE 1.0: Once past Island No. 8, cross straight to **Government Island**. Turn and paddle northwest along the shore of the island.

MILE 1.5: There is a campsite with picnic tables and trash cans at the north tip of the island. If you are not paddling any farther, return by the same route. If you are paddling around the island, head southeast along the shore.

MILE 2.5: There is a second camping area on the point, with a cobblestone beach. Though this is a nice spot, it is somewhat less sheltered than the one at the north end of the island. Continue paddling to the southeast. *Caution:* After leaving the campsite, you will be exposed to southerly and southeasterly winds. Wait for good weather before paddling this section.

MILES 3.0–4.0: **Penny Island** is actually joined to Government Island by a long, thin gravel spit. Although landing is possible in calm weather, the numerous boulders and shoals are difficult to negotiate in rough weather. After you round Penny Island, turn and paddle northwest along the shore. *Caution:* Once around the point you will also be exposed to southwesterly winds. This shoreline is very poor for landing a kayak except in calm weather.

MILE 4.5: At the end of the bay formed by Government Island and **La Salle Islands**, there is a pleasant sand beach with a campsite set back in the woods. Though maps show a very narrow channel between the islands, when we visited, it was not passable without a portage because of the low water level. Higher water may allow paddlers to slip through, and if it is so, you can reach the north island by this route.

MILES 4.5–9.0: If the channel is not deep enough, return to the north side of the island and then back to the launch site by the same route. *Sidetrip:* If you are camping on Government Island and have time for more paddling, try a sidetrip to Les Cheneaux Channel. There are some older boathouses and cottages from the days when this area could only be accessed by boat. (This can also be done as a day trip from the Lakeshore Drive boat launch.) There are several possible ways to get there, but if you paddle to the north end of La Salle Island from the north end of Government Island, then to Connors Point and the Cheneaux Channel and back by the same route, the round-trip distance is 10–12 miles.

Where to Eat & Where to Stay

RESTAURANTS & LODGING The **Islands Inn** (906–484–2293) is located near the junction of M 134 and M 129 in Cedarville. There are a few other motels in the area, but most of the lodging seems to be rental cottages. Call Les Cheneaux Chamber of Commerce for a list at (906) 484–3935.

CAMPING If you are looking for camping on the mainland, try **Loons Point Campground** on Cedarville Bay. Call (906) 484–2881 for information.

Lake Erie, Lake Saint Clair, & the Detroit River

Route 20:

Harsens Island

T he Saint Clair River empties into Lake Saint Clair through a group of islands, marshes, and channels called the Saint Clair Flats. The sheltered waters of the Saint Clair Flats Wildlife Area are perfect for beginning paddlers who want to explore this landscape. Paddling through beds of wild rice, cattails, and fragmites, kayakers have many opportunities for viewing waterfowl and wading birds. Intermediate paddlers who want to leave the shelter of Little Muscamoot Bay can also explore the Old Channel Light. The old stone lighthouse tower rises from a shoal at the mouth of Big Muscamoot Bay, about 0.75 mile from the nearest land.

TRIP HIGHLIGHTS: A historic lighthouse; extensive wetlands with cattails, fragmites and wild rice beds; great bird watching.

TRIP RATING:
Beginner: 4–5 mile loop around Little Muscamoot Bay.
Intermediate: 10 mile round-trip from the boat ramp at Little Muscamoot Bay to the Old Channel Light and back.

TRIP DURATION: Day trip.

NAVIGATION AIDS: NOAA chart 14850; USGS: *Lake Saint Clair* (42082-E1) at 1:100,000.

CAUTIONS: Shallow water may produce breaking waves far from shore. It is easy to get lost in the maze of channels and islands, and the land features will change with even small fluctuations in lake level. Cold water in spring or fall.

TRIP PLANNING: Always check the marine forecast before heading out. Winds from the southwest could produce large waves at the mouth of Big Muscamoot Bay, but Little Muscamoot Bay is well sheltered. In spring or fall the water can be very cold and a dry suit or wet suit is recommended. Plan your trip so you return to the launch site in daylight because it is easy to get lost in the marsh at night. In summer the main channels can be busy with small craft and "pestilent" watercraft (e.g., Jet Skis), but in a kayak you can glide into shallow marsh areas where these craft can't follow.

LAUNCH SITE: From the town of Algonac, take the ferry to Harsens Island (the fee is $5.00 round-trip). From the ferry turn right (west) on Highway 154, which becomes North Channel Drive. Follow North Channel Drive until it feeds onto Golf Drive and continue until it dead-ends at Middle Channel Drive. Turn left onto Middle Channel Drive and follow it west along the Middle Channel. The first public boat ramp accesses an inland marsh area, so continue on past it, until you cross a bridge over a small channel, then turn left into the boat ramp access for Little Muscamoot Bay. There is parking and an outhouse, but no potable water is available. There is a small convenience store and bait shop about 1 mile farther down Middle Channel Drive.

DIRECTIONS

START: From the **boat landing**, turn left **(N 42° 35.14', W 082° 38.05')** to go around a small marshy island covered with fragmites stalks 8–10 feet high. If you take the channel in the other direction, you will likely run aground. After clearing the small island, head south along the narrow channel toward Little Muscamoot Bay.

MILE 0.5: **(N 42° 34.77', W 082° 38.22')**. At the end of the narrow channel, you come to a small building along a low sheet-piling shore. Memorize this spot so you can find the entrance to the channel back to the boat ramp. You have now entered **Little Muscamoot Bay**.

MILE 1.0: As you head south into Little Muscamoot Bay, you follow a long, narrow point that at higher water levels is broken into several islands with channels in between them. At Mile 1.0 you reach the end of the point. Beginners who want to stay in Little Muscamoot Bay should turn left, heading east to circle the bay counterclockwise for a 5-mile loop in sheltered waters. Intermediate paddlers who want to explore Big

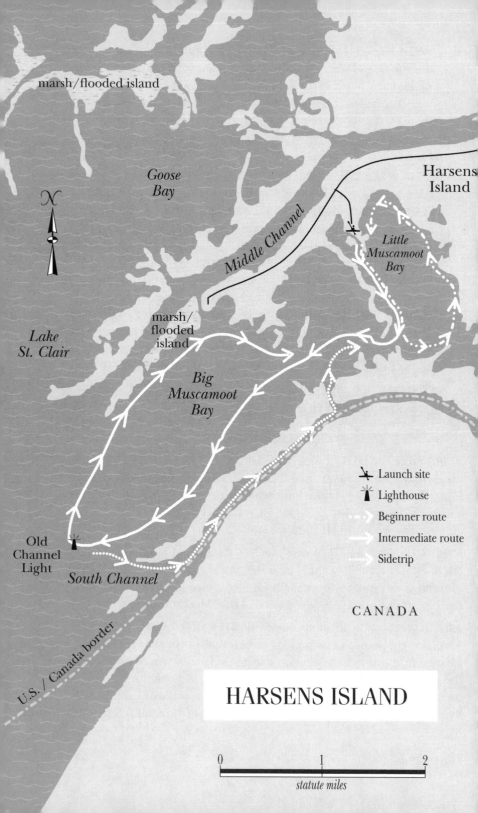

marsh/flooded island

*Goose
Bay*

Middle Channel

Harsens
Island

N

*Little
Muscamoot
Bay*

*Lake
St. Clair*

marsh/
flooded
island

*Big
Muscamoot
Bay*

Old
Channel
Light

South Channel

U.S. / Canada border

CANADA

Launch site

Lighthouse

Beginner route

Intermediate route

Sidetrip

HARSENS ISLAND

0   1   2

statute miles

Muscamoot Bay and the Old Channel Light should round the point to the right and head southwest.

MILE 2.0: After rounding the point you enter a shallow area of the bay with extensive beds of wild rice. The stalks are spaced widely enough so that you can glide through this huge bed of reeds without them greatly impeding your progress. At about Mile 2.0 the rice beds end, and you enter the open waters of **Big Muscamoot Bay**.

MILE 5.0: Continue paddling southwest along the south shore of Big Muscamoot Bay along the low island that separates the bay from the South Channel. About 0.75 mile from the tip of this long finger of land is **Old Channel Light**. You can paddle out to this weather-worn old relic. The stone tower is still standing although the light is no longer in service—the new light is visible farther offshore. *Caution:* The lighthouse sits on a small cobble and boulder shoal, so land here only in calm weather. To complete your trip you can retrace your route and return along the north side of the bay, or you can head south into the South Channel and return north through the small channel that connects the South Channel to Big Muscamoot Bay. *Caution:* If you return via the South Channel, stay near shore to avoid boat traffic.

Where to Eat & Where to Stay

RESTAURANTS For information on restaurants in the Algonac area call the Algonac Chamber of Commerce at (810) 794–5511. If you are heading back west on Highway 29, you may want to stop at the **North Channel Brewing Company** (810–948–BEER). This brewpub is located about 10 miles west of Algonac. They have good food as well as beer. **LODGING & CAMPING** For lodging in the Algonac area, call the Algonac Chamber of Commerce at (810) 794–5511.

Route 21:

------- ------- ------- ------- ------- ------- -------- ➤

Windsor/Detroit: Belle Isle & Peche Island

Mention the Detroit River to most people and visions of the urban waterfront or the industrial monstrosities of the River Rouge area come to mind. Wildlife and island parks are not likely to make the list. Located in the Detroit River just downstream of Lake Saint Clair, Peche Island is a provincial park that provides quite literally an island of wilderness between the cities of Windsor and Detroit. In the near future the city of Windsor will likely take control of the island as a city park, but it will be left wild and undeveloped regardless. Belle Isle is connected to Detroit by a bridge, is more developed, and gets far more use than Peche Island. Belle Isle was purchased by Detroit in 1879, and this city park was designed by landscape architect Fredrick Law Olmstead, who also designed Central Park in New York City. Attractions on Belle Isle include a maritime museum, zoo, aquarium, swimming beach, fountain, Coast Guard station, and marina. The Detroit River is also a great place for boat-watchers. All ships that travel between Lake Huron and Lake Erie pass between Peche Island and Belle Isle.

TRIP HIGHLIGHTS: Great boat watching in busy shipping channel, bird watching, great urban views, two island parks to explore.

TRIP RATING:
Intermediate: 11-mile loop around both islands.

TRIP DURATION: Day trip.

NAVIGATION AIDS: NOAA chart 14848; USGS: *Belle Isle* and *Detroit* (7.5 minute).

CAUTIONS: The route crosses a busy shipping lane, current of 2–3 knots midchannel, submerged dock posts and other shallow bottom hazards, cold water in spring and fall.

TRIP PLANNING: Always check the marine forecast before heading out. Although relatively sheltered, easterly winds could bring swells from Lake Saint Clair. The river current and human-made shoreline features, such as concrete rip-rap and sheet piling, can produce confused seas from even small swells. Start early enough so you can avoid crossing the shipping channel at night.

LAUNCH SITE: Detroit has largely ignored the recreational potential of the river, and much of the shore is sheet piling or industrial docks, which are not suited for launching kayaks. The Canadian side of the river, with its many waterfront parks, is a much better habitat for kayakers. Although you can launch from the Landview Park Marina boat ramp, local paddlers prefer to launch for free from a small city park access that they have named Kayak Cove. From Detroit cross the river via the Ambassador Bridge and turn left on College (east), then left on California (north) to Riverside. Follow Riverside east along the river until you see a lighthouse (the Old Point Pelee Light), which marks the entrance to the Landview Park Marina. Just past the marina watch for the Lilly Kaziley's restaurant on the left and a city park parking lot on the right. Turn right into the lot and carry boats across the street to the small sand beach where someone has planted a sign, KAYAK COVE. There are no bathroom facilities or potable water, although you can use the washrooms at the restaurant.

DIRECTIONS

START: From **Kayak Cove (N 42° 20.36', W 082° 55.61')** head north and cross to the north end of **Peche Island**. Peche Island has an interesting history, originally starting out as a fishing camp, hence the name Peche, which is "fish" in French. The island was privately owned for a time by the Walker family, owners of the Windsor distillery that makes Canadian

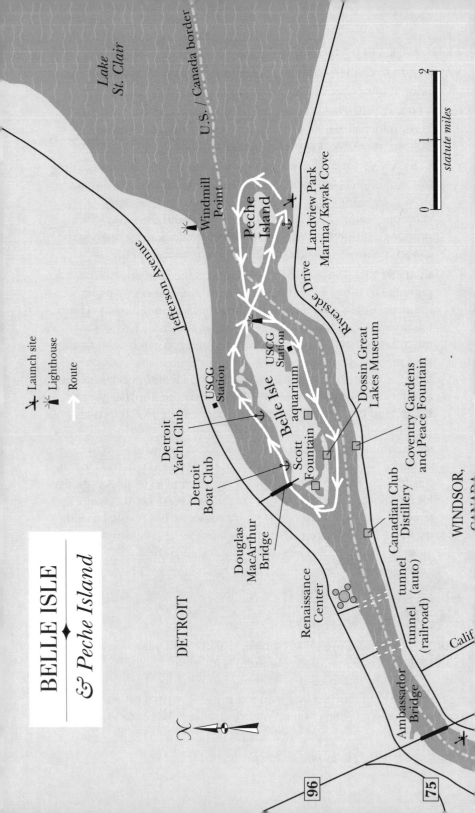

BELLE ISLE
& Peche Island

Lake
St. Clair

U.S. / Canada border

Windmill
Point

Peche
Island

Landview Park
Marina/Kayak Cove

Jefferson Avenue

Riverside Drive

USCG
Station

Detroit
Yacht Club

USCG
Station

Belle Isle

aquarium

Dossin Great
Lakes Museum

Detroit
Boat Club

Scott
Fountain

Coventry Gardens
and Peace Fountain

Douglas
MacArthur
Bridge

Canadian Club
Distillery

WINDSOR,
CANADA

Renaissance
Center

tunnel
(auto)

tunnel
(railroad)

Calif

Ambassador
Bridge

DETROIT

96

75

⚓ Launch site
✳ Lighthouse
⬆ Route

N

0   1   2
statute miles

Club whiskey. Having a distillery in Canada less than 1.0 mile from the United States during Prohibition was good business, and countless cases of Canadian whiskey undoubtedly made their way across the Detroit River on rum-runner boats under the cover of darkness.

MILE 0.5: After reaching Peche Island continue north and around the east end of the island. *Caution:* On the east end of the island, there is a line of submerged dock posts near shore.

MILE 1.5: Paddling west down the wooded shores of the north side of Peche Island, you pass several narrow sand beaches—good places to stop and take a break or a swim. At Mile 1.5 you come to the end of the island. From here you make the 0.75-mile crossing to the **Livingstone Memorial Light** at the east tip of Belle Isle. *Caution:* All of the shipping traffic passes between Peche Island and Belle Isle. You have a clear view up and down river, so make sure you have an opening in the shipping traffic before attempting to cross.

MILE 2.25: On reaching the Livingstone Memorial Light, head south and west along the south side of Belle Isle. Remember that the shipping lanes are just a short distance offshore. By paddling farther from shore, you can take advantage of a 2-knot current, but you need to keep your eyes open to steer clear of ships if you are not skimming along the shore.

MILE 4.0: Paddling down the south shore, watch out for the concrete debris used to control erosion along the shore. Apparently former Mayor Coleman Young thought that ugly jagged concrete debris was just the ticket to protect the Belle Isle shoreline. In spite of the unfriendly concrete erosion control measures, most of Belle Isle is quite beautiful. After about 2.0 miles of paddling along the south shore of the island, you come to the Belle Isle Aquarium, Belle Isle Coast Guard Station, and the Dossin Great Lakes Museum.

MILE 5.25: At approximately Mile 5.25, you reach the west tip of the island. Turn the corner and head upstream along the north side of the island. By staying near shore and returning along the north side of the island, the current you'll encounter is less than one knot.

MILE 5.75: About 0.50 mile upstream from the western tip of the island, you pass the Detroit City Police boat docks on Belle Isle. Just upstream from the police docks is the **Douglas MacArthur Bridge**, which connects Belle Isle to downtown Detroit. Just upstream of the bridge is the abandoned marina of the old **Detroit Boat Club**.

MILE 6.75: Heading upstream along the north shore of Belle Isle, you pass the Belle Isle Swimming Beach and come to the **Detroit Yacht Club**, which is an active marina. *Caution:* Watch for small craft traffic here.

MILE 8.25: Continuing east from the Detroit Yacht Club, you come to a series of channels and small islands owned by the Detroit City Water Department. At about Mile 8.25 you are at the eastern tip of Belle Isle. From here you will cross east 0.75 mile to Peche Island. *Caution:* All of the shipping traffic passes between Peche Island and Belle Isle. You have a clear view up and down river, so make sure you have an opening in the shipping traffic before attempting to cross.

MILE 9.75: After reaching the west end of Peche Island, follow the south shore of the island east. About 0.75 mile down the south shore of the island you can head inland through marshy channels to explore a small wetland area, which is a good spot for bird watching.

MILE 10.5: From Peche Island head south to make the 0.3-mile crossing to the south shore of the Detroit River. Then turn east to return to Kayak Cove.

Where to Eat & Where to Stay

R E S T A U R A N T S   Lilly Kazily's is a great choice because it is right next to Kayak Cove, has good food, and best of all an outside deck where dripping wet kayakers in stinky neoprene may dine. Windsor has many dining opportunities, including many excellent ethnic restaurants in the various immigrant neighborhoods. For information call the Windsor Convention and Visitors Bureau at (800) 265–3633. **L O D G I N G & C A M P I N G**   Windsor has many lodging and some camping options. For information call the Windsor Convention and Visitors Bureau.

Route 22:

━ ━ ━ ━ ━ ━ ━ ━ ━ ━ ━ ━ ━ ━ ━ ━ ━ ➤

Windsor/Detroit: Kayak Cove to the Ambassador Bridge

T his trip also combines great views of the Detroit and Windsor waterfront with a chance to explore the two island parks, Belle Isle and Peche Island (see Rte. 21). As you travel from Kayak Cove on the Detroit River, you will pass not only the two island parks, but several Windsor waterfront parks, including Coventry Gardens and the International Peace Fountain. The International Peace Fountain is a giant floating fountain located in the river near Coventry Gardens in Windsor. In summer the fountain pumps 15,000 gallons per minute and shoots streams of water 70 feet in the air, with pulsating jets and colored lights. I researched the route too late in the season to see it, but I have it on good authority that it is great fun for kayakers—almost as much fun as it was running through the sprinkler as a kid! Past the islands you paddle along the core of downtown Detroit, including the Renaissance Center, a group of tall modern buildings eighty-one stories high, covered with forty-two acres of glass.

TRIP HIGHLIGHTS: Great boat watching in busy shipping channel, bird watching, great urban views, two island parks to explore, a giant floating fountain.

TRIP RATING:
Intermediate: 9-mile trip from Kayak Cove to the Ambassador Bridge one way.

TRIP DURATION: Day trip.

NAVIGATION AIDS: NOAA chart 14848; USGS: *Belle Isle* and *Detroit* (7.5 minute).

CAUTIONS: The route crosses a busy shipping lane, current of 2–3 knots midchannel, submerged dock posts, and other shallow bottom hazards; cold water in spring and fall.

TRIP PLANNING: Always check the marine forecast before heading out. Although the route is relatively sheltered, easterly winds could bring swells from Lake Saint Clair. The river current and human-made shoreline features, such as concrete rip-rap and sheet piling, can produce confused seas from even small swells. Start early enough so you can avoid crossing the shipping channel at night. Although this could be paddled as an out-and-back trip from Kayak Cove, it would be a difficult fight against the current on the return trip unless you stayed very close to shore.

LAUNCH SITES: Kayak Cove: See Rte. 21.

Chewitt Beach: From Riverside Drive (See directions to Kayak Cove, Rte. 21), head west toward the Ambassador Bridge. As you pass under the bridge, Riverside becomes Sandwich Street. Just past the bridge you come to the intersection of Sandwich and Chewitt (No, really, those are the street names—not my pun, someone else's). Turn right on Chewitt to the free municipal beach and boat ramp. There are no bathrooms or potable water available at the ramp, but there is parking and a nice sand beach to land kayaks. Please note that this boat ramp does not appear on most city or provincial maps.

DIRECTIONS

START: From **Kayak Cove (N 42° 20.36', W 082° 55.61')** head north and cross to the south shore of Peche Island. Peche Island originally started out as a fishing camp—hence the name Peche, French for "fish."

MILE 0.5: After crossing to Peche Island, turn west and paddle along the south shore. At Mile 0.5 there is a small bay where you can explore the marsh areas and sheltered channels that lead into the island.

MILE 1.25: Continuing along the south side of Peche Island, you'll pass wooded shoreline reaching the west end of the island at Mile 1.25.

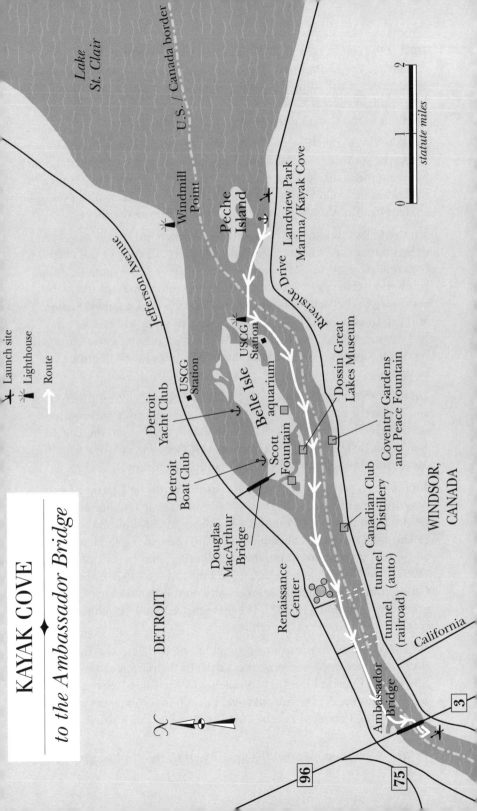

KAYAK COVE

to the Ambassador Bridge

DETROIT

WINDSOR, CANADA

Launch site
Lighthouse
Route

Lake St. Clair

U.S. / Canada border

Windmill Point

Peche Island

Jefferson Avenue

Riverside Drive

Landview Park
Marina / Kayak Cove

Detroit Yacht Club

USCG Station

Belle Isle

aquarium

USCG Station

Dossin Great Lakes Museum

Detroit Boat Club

Scott Fountain

Coventry Gardens and Peace Fountain

Douglas MacArthur Bridge

Canadian Club Distillery

Renaissance Center

tunnel (auto)

tunnel (railroad)

California

Ambassador Bridge

96

75

3

0   1   2
statute miles

MILE 2.0: From the end of Peche Island, you make the 0.75-mile crossing to the **Livingstone Memorial Light** at the east tip of Belle Isle. *Caution:* All of the shipping traffic passes between Peche Island and Belle Isle. You have a clear view up and down river, so make sure you have an opening in the shipping traffic before attempting to cross.

MILE 2.25: On reaching the Livingstone Memorial Light, head west along the south side of Belle Isle. Remember that the shipping lanes are just a short distance offshore. By paddling farther from shore you can take advantage of a 2-knot current, but you need to keep your eyes open to steer clear of ships if you are not skimming along the shore.

MILE 4.0: Paddling down the south shore watch out for the concrete debris used to control erosion along the shore. In spite of the unfriendly concrete erosion control measures most of Belle Isle is quite beautiful. After about 2.0 miles of paddling along the south shore of the island, you come to the **Belle Isle Aquarium, Belle Isle Coast Guard Station,** and the **Dossin Great Lakes Museum.** To the south you can see the International Peace Fountain near Windsor's Coventry Park. On a hot day some kayakers may want to cross over to play in the floating fountain!

MILE 5.25: At approximately Mile 5.25, you reach the west tip of Belle Isle. Cross the channel north to north bank of the river and continue downstream on the Detroit side. Note that in addition to the USCG station on Belle Isle, the main **Detroit USCG** station is across from the western tip of Belle Isle on the mainland Detroit shore.

MILE 6.0: As you paddle along the north bank of the Detroit River, you pass the core of downtown Detroit. Several historic buildings can be viewed from the water: Penobscot Building (1928), Buhl Building (1925), and the Guardian Building (1929). Also along the waterfront are several more modern buildings, including One Detroit Center (1992), Madden Building (1987), Joe Louis Arena (1979), and the Cobo Center and Arena. At Mile 6.0 you come to the Renaissance Center, which was completed in 1977. It is an eighty-one-story building complex covered with forty-two acres of glass.

MILE 8.5: As you continue downstream along the Detroit side of the river, the shore becomes more industrial. In the distance down river, you can see the massive industrial complexes by the River Rouge. At Mile 8.5 you come to the Ambassador Bridge. From here cross south under the bridge to the Canadian side of the river. The current is strong, running

2–3 knots at midchannel, so you may have to point your bow into the current to front ferry across. *Caution:* All of the shipping traffic between Lake Huron and Lake Erie passes through the Detroit River—be careful crossing this very busy shipping lane.

MILE 9.0: After crossing to the Canadian side, paddle just downstream of the bridge to the boat ramp at **Chewitt Beach (N 42° 18.39', W 083° 04.57')**.

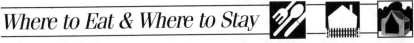

Where to Eat & Where to Stay

RESTAURANTS, LODGING & CAMPING See Route 21: Windsor/Detroit: Belle Isle & Peche Island.

Route 23:

━━ ━━ ━━ ━━ ━━ ━━ ━━ ━━ ━━ ━━ ━━ ━━ ➡

Point Pelee National Park

Point Pelee National Park contains one of the last large freshwater marshes on the Great Lakes. In all 8 square miles of park land protects a variety of habitat for wildlife, including open fields, forests, marshes, ponds, and sand beaches. Point Pelee is the southernmost tip of mainland Canada, and its southern location, coupled with the moderating influence of Lake Erie, ensure a warmer climate than in almost any other part of Canada. This moderate climate allows many plants and animals that are not normally found in Canada to thrive within the park. The point extends far south into the lake, a natural crossing point for migratory birds flying north or south across Lake Erie. The incredible bird watching brings visitors from all over the world, with over 400,000 visitors enjoying the park each year. The forests of Point Pelee were first set aside under British rule in the 1790s as a naval reserve to save virgin stands of oak and white pine for ship building. In spite of the naval reserve, squatters moved in to use the point for farming and fishing. The passage between Point Pelee and Pelee Island is the most treacherous passage on the Great Lakes, having shallow water and many shoals. Since the mid-1800s over 275 ships have been lost in the Pelee Passage. In 1902 a lifesaving station was established at the tip of the point and remained operational until the 1930s. In 1918 Point Pelee became Canada's ninth national park. Today the park's boundaries are identical to those of the naval reserve of the 1790s.

TRIP HIGHLIGHTS: Fantastic bird watching, hiking trails, sand beaches, unique wildlife in a southern microclimate.

TRIP RATING:

Beginner: 4–5 mile loop through the marsh (West Cranberry Pond and Lake Pond).

Intermediate/Advanced: 11-mile loop from the Marsh Boardwalk to the Northwest Beach (includes a 0.3-mile walk from one launch site to the other).

TRIP DURATION: Day trip.

NAVIGATION AIDS: CHS chart 2123; Canadian topographic maps 40 J/2 and 40 G/15 at 1:50,000.

CAUTIONS: Shallow water in the Pelee Passage of Lake Erie can produce very steep waves with sudden storms, the long point produces long-shore currents and rip tides at the tip (many swimmers and waders have died off the tip of the point); cold water in spring and fall.

TRIP PLANNING: Always check the marine forecast before heading out. Strong winds from any direction but north can produce large steep surf. The long point and shallow water can produce strong rip currents and steep chaotic waves; it should only be rounded in calm weather unless you have advanced skills. With strong winds you can choose to paddle on the sheltered side or explore the sheltered marsh area. Lake Erie is relatively warm in summer, but for spring and fall paddling a wet suit or dry suit is strongly recommended.

LAUNCH SITES:

Marsh Boardwalk: To get to the park, follow Highway 3 to Leamington, then follow the park signs (brown signs with the outline of a beaver) to the national park. The signs are small and easy to miss—watch carefully so you don't miss any turns. About 1.5 miles south of the park entrance, watch for the signs directing you to the Marsh Boardwalk. There is a parking lot, canoe landing, and observation tower on the edge of the marsh and small inland lakes. It is helpful to climb the observation tower to scout your route east through the marsh channel to Lake Erie. Washrooms and potable water are available. There is also a small food concession.

Northwest Beach: To get to the park follow Highway 3 to Leamington and then follow the park signs (brown signs with the

Point Pelee National Park

outline of a beaver) to the national park. About 1.5 miles south of the park entrance, watch for the signs directing you to the Northwest Beach picnic area. From the parking lot to the sand beach on the west side of the peninsula is a 200 foot walk over level ground. Washrooms and potable water are available.

DIRECTIONS

START: From **Marsh Boardwalk (N 41° 58.09', W 082° 31.84')** canoe landing, follow the weedy channel along the boardwalk then head east toward the open water of the Lake Pond.

MILE 1.5: At about Mile 0.5 the narrow weedy marsh channel empties into the open waters of the **Lake Pond**. On windy days paddlers can explore the shores of the Lake Pond and West Cranberry Pond. Heading east across the Lake Pond, you come to a narrow sandbar at Mile 1.5, where it is only a short portage of about 150 feet to **Lake Erie (N 41° 57.92', W 082° 30.21')**. Beginning paddlers can explore the sheltered waters of the marsh and inland lakes or portage for a short paddle on the east shore of the peninsula before returning to the

Marsh Boardwalk canoe landing. Weather permitting intermediate and advanced paddlers continue south down the east side of the peninsula.

MILES 1.5–3.0: Heading south you paddle along a narrow sand and gravel beach with a narrow, wooded strip of land separating the marsh from Lake Erie.

MILE 4.0: After Mile 3.0 the narrow strip of land and the large marsh end, and you follow a narrow sand beach and wooded shoreline. At Mile 4.0 you come to wooden dock posts from an old pier.

MILE 6.0: At Mile 6.0 you come to the tip of **Point Pelee (N 41° 54.45', W**

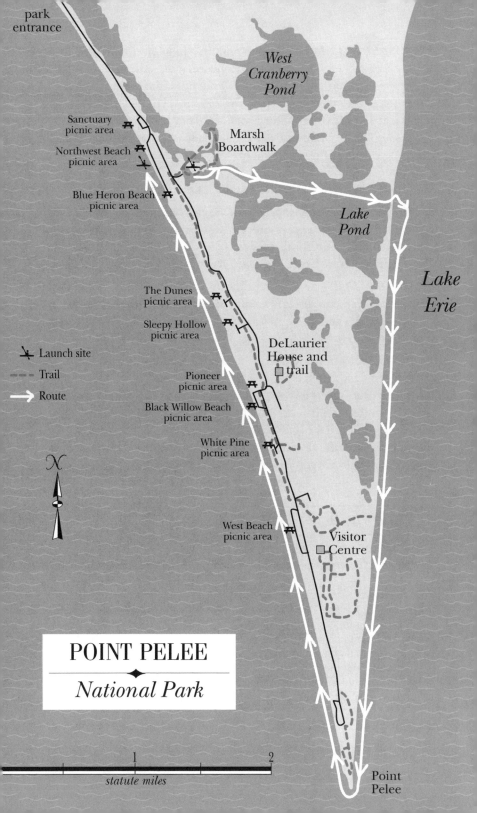

park
entrance

*West
Cranberry
Pond*

Marsh
Boardwalk

*Lake
Pond*

*Lake
Erie*

Sanctuary
picnic area

Northwest Beach
picnic area

Blue Heron Beach
picnic area

The Dunes
picnic area

Sleepy Hollow
picnic area

DeLaurier
House and
trail

Pioneer
picnic area

Black Willow Beach
picnic area

White Pine
picnic area

West Beach
picnic area

Visitor
Centre

Launch site

Trail

Route

N

Point
Pelee

POINT PELEE
National Park

1   2
statute miles

082° 30.54'). The low sand point ends in a long sandbar that reaches far out into Lake Erie. Near the tip is a hiking trail, washrooms, and a phone. A lifesaving station was established at the tip of the point to rescue ships that ran aground while trying to make it through the treacherous Pelee Passage. The lifesaving station operated from 1902 until the 1930s. *Caution:* The tip of Point Pelee often produces strong rip currents. Expect steep waves and choppy conditions off the point, especially if waves are running against a rip current. If weather conditions permit, round the point and head north up the west side of the point.

*MILE **7.75:*** Narrow sand beaches continue up the west side of the peninsula, with the exception of a short section of limestone blocks installed to prevent shore erosion. About 1.75 miles north from the tip, you come to **West Beach** and just inland is the park **Visitor Centre**.

*MILES **8.0–10.0:*** The sand beach shore continues with several day access beach and picnic sites: **White Pine, Black Willow Beach, Pioneer, Sleepy Hollow,** and **The Dunes**. All of these sites have parking, washrooms, and easy access to the beach, making them suitable launch or take-out sites.

*MILE **11.0:*** Continuing north you pass **Blue Heron Beach** and come to the **Northwest Beach (N 41° 58.24' W 082° 32.20')**. You can end your trip here and retrieve your car from the Marsh Boardwalk parking lot by making a 0.3-mile trip on foot. As you walk you are retracing a historical portage route used by the early settlers and Native Canadians. To avoid canoeing around the long point and the risk of the dangerous currents and chaotic seas at the tip of the point, early travelers would make this short portage and pass through the marsh into Lake Erie.

Where to Eat & Where to Stay

RESTAURANTS   At the Marsh Boardwalk canoe landing, there is a small food concession stand for a quick bite to eat called the **Cattail Café** (519–322–1654). Just north of the park is **Paula's Fish Place** (519–326–1292), a family restaurant that specializes in fresh fish. For excellent seafood in the town of Leamington try **The Dock** restaurant. For information on restaurants in the area, call Leamington Tourist Information at (800) 250–3336. **LODGING**   The town of Leamington has many lodging options. For information call Leamington Tourist Information. **CAMPING**   With the exception of special event group camping, there is no camping within Pelee National Park. Camping is available east of the point at **Wheatley Provincial Park** (519–825–4659). For private campgrounds in the area, call Leamington Tourist Information at (800) 250–3336.

Route 24:

―――― ―――― ―――― ―――― ―――― ―――― ―→

Pelee Island

South of Point Pelee and north of Sandusky, Ohio, is Pelee Island. This 10,000-acre island is the largest island in Lake Erie, and the southernmost land area in Canada. This quiet rural community has a year-round population of 275 people and a summer population of about 1,000. The island is not a wilderness island although it does have nature reserves on its northern and southern tips. Seen from the air the island looks like a quilt; most of the land area is devoted to crops and vineyards. As with Point Pelee, the southern latitude and the moderating effects of Lake Erie make the climate very mild. Many southern plant and animal species found here are not found elsewhere in Canada. Located near the U.S.-Canada border at the southernmost end of the Pelee Passage, the island has an interesting history, from shipwrecks to Prohibition-era rumrunners.

TRIP HIGHLIGHTS: Bird watching, sand beaches, unique wildlife in a southern microclimate, winery tours, and a historic lighthouse.

TRIP RATING:
Intermediate: 24-mile loop around the island, starting and ending at West Dock.

TRIP DURATION: Overnight trip.

NAVIGATION AIDS: CHS chart 2123, Canadian topographic maps 40 G/10 and 40 G/15 at 1:50,000.

CAUTIONS: Shallow water in the Pelee Passage of Lake Erie can produce very steep waves with sudden storms; the long point at

Fish Point produces long-shore currents and rip tides at its tip; cold water in spring and fall.

TRIP PLANNING: Make reservations for the ferry in advance by calling (800) 661–2220. The ferry service runs from March through November. From either Leamington or Kingsville, Ontario, you can take the ferry for $7.50 Canadian per adult and $16.50 Canadian for your car (1998 prices). If you are not bringing a car to the island, you will have to make freight arrangements for your kayak(s). The crossing time is about 1.5 hours from Ontario. Advanced kayakers can make the long crossing from the mainland, but we don't recommend it because the shallow waters of the Pelee Passage can become very rough with any sudden change of the weather. Once on the island always check the weather before starting. There is no wilderness camping on the island, so make arrangements for camping or cottage rentals in advance of your trip.

LAUNCH SITES: The ferry docks are easy to find with signs in each town to direct you. From Ontario you can leave from Leamington (at the foot of Erie Street S.), or Kingsville (Kingsville Government Dock off Park Street). In the United States you depart from Sandusky, Ohio (at the foot of Jackson Street). All ferries arrive at the West Dock on Pelee Island.

DIRECTIONS

START: Crossing by ferry from the mainland you arrive at **West Dock** on Pelee Island. Most of the city offices and stores on Pelee Island are located near the West Dock. A good place to start your trip is a visit to the **Pelee Island Heritage Centre**, located close to the ferry dock. A visit to this museum will give you an appreciation for the history of the island and make your trip around the island more interesting. About 1.0 mile away is the **Pelee Island Winery Pavillion**, which has shuttle buses running for free from the West Dock. The winery offers tours, wine tasting, and an outdoor barbecue lunch. To start your circumnavigation of the island, head south and paddle along the west coast.

MILE 2.5: Paddling south down the west side of the island you pass along an unfriendly shore of limestone block that was installed for erosion control. At Mile 2.5 you come to the start of the **Fish Point**

Pelee Island

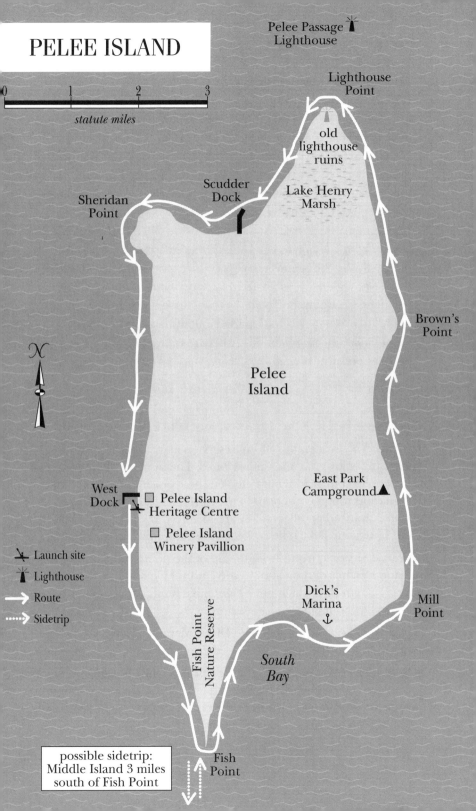

"A Colorful History"

Middle Island is privately owned, so please respect the owners property rights. The island has a colorful history and previous owners included Al Capone's accountant, and Bonnie and Clyde's driver C. W. Moss. Located near the U.S.-Canada border, it made an ideal location for rumrunners during Prohibition. On the south side of the island is an old hotel. Keep your eyes open for old abandoned cars with skis on the front—in winter rumrunners used these homemade snowmobiles to smuggle liquor from Canada to the United States across the ice. Before the Civil War the island was part of the underground railroad, which smuggled slaves north to Canada. During the Civil War a group of Confederate soldiers escaped from a prison camp and made their way north to Canada via Middle Island. Today the island is largely uninhabited—with the exception of a huge population of nesting gulls, herons, and cormorants.

Nature Reserve. Here the shore becomes sand beach.

MILE 4.0: The Fish Point Nature Reserve is a great place for bird-watchers to enjoy gulls and wading birds. The sand beach ends in a long, narrow point similar to Point Pelee on the mainland. *Caution:* Strong rip currents and rough conditions may be present at the tip of the points. *Sidetrip:* Advanced paddlers may want to consider a sidetrip to Middle Island by making a 3.0-mile crossing south from the tip of the point.

MILE 5.5: Heading north from the tip of the point, you continue along the sand beaches of the nature reserve until Mile 5.5. You are now entering **South Bay**, which has a lagoonlike pond and marsh area, also good for bird watching.

MILE 7.0: At Mile 7.0 you come to **Dick's Marina**, which has a private campground, bathrooms, and showers.

MILE 8.5: From the marina continue east then turn north to round **Mill Point**. Along the shore of Mill Point, there are low shelves of limestone rock. As you continue north from the point, the limestone shore ends, and you pass cottages and sandy beaches.

MILE 10.0: At Mile 10.0 you come to a public sand beach. Across from the beach is the **East Park Campground**, a Pelee Township campground with twenty-five sites.

MILE 14.0: Paddling up the east side of the island, the sand beach shores and private cottages continue. At Mile 14.0 you reach the southern edge of the **Lighthouse Point Nature Reserve**. Inside the nature reserve is the **Lake Henry Marsh**, an excellent area for bird-watchers.

MILE 16.0: At Mile 16.0 you reach the end of **Lighthouse Point**. Offshore to the north of the point is the **Pelee Passage Lighthouse**, which has replaced the old Pelee Island Light. Make sure you explore the ruins of the old lighthouse. Its stone tower still stands. The old light began service in 1834, the oldest lighthouse on Lake Erie.

MILE 18.0: Rounding the point and turning south, you paddle along the sand beaches of the west side of Lighthouse Point for about 1.5 miles. At Mile 18.0 you come to the north dock, also known as **Scudder Dock**. Near the dock are a marina, restaurant, and cottages.

MILE 19.5: Heading west from Scudder Dock, you come to **Sheridan Point**. Round the point and head south down the west side of Pelee Island.

MILE 23.5: Continue south down the west side of the island to finish the circumnavigation at the West Dock.

Where to Eat & Where to Stay

RESTAURANTS   For excellent seafood in the town of Leamington, try **The Dock** restaurant. For information on restaurants on the mainland and Pelee Island, call Leamington Tourist Information at (800) 250–3336. Pelee Island is a resort area with many dining options. For information on restaurants on Pelee Island write Public Relations, Pelee Island, Ontario N0R 1M0 Canada. **LODGING**   For lodging information on the mainland and Pelee Island, you can call Leamington Tourist Information. On Pelee Island there are many cottages and motels on or near the water. For information you can write Public Relations. **CAMPING**   There are two campgrounds near the water's edge on Pelee Island, one at **Dick's Marina** on South Bay (519–724–2024), and the other, Pelee Township's **East Park Campground** (519–724–2470). For camping on the mainland call Leamington Tourist Information.

Route 25:

Rondeau Provincial Park

The name Rondeau comes from the French, ronde eau, meaning "round water." The park is aptly named—the long peninsula of park land is divided by only a narrow channel from a second peninusla to form a snug harbor of round water. The land was first set aside by the British government as Ordinance Land by Lord Simcoe in 1795 and was used as a naval repair station during the War of 1812. In 1894 Rondeau became the second provincial park in Ontario. Today you can enjoy the same sand beaches, low coastal sand dunes, extensive marshes, and Carolinian forests that visitors have enjoyed for over one hundred years. The forests, beaches, and cattail marshes are ideal for bird watching, with 80 percent of all Ontario bird species being sighted within the park boundaries. There are also a number of rare plants found in the park, including nineteen species of orchids.

TRIP HIGHLIGHTS: Bird watching, hiking trails, sand beaches, unique wildlife in a southern microclimate, exploring narrow channels in a cattail marsh.

TRIP RATING:
Beginner/Intermediate: 12-mile trip one-way from the Rondeau Park dock to Lake Erie Beach near the Visitor Centre.

TRIP DURATION: Day trip.

NAVIGATION AIDS: CHS chart 2122, Canadian topographic map 40 I/5 at 1:50,000.

CAUTIONS: Winds from the south or east can cause large surf; small changes in water levels can greatly change the shape of the

shoreline or make channels in the marsh too shallow to be passable; clapotis off the sheet piling at the harbor entrance; cold water in spring and fall.

TRIP PLANNING: Always check the marine forecast before starting your trip. When parking a shuttle car at the Lake Erie takeout, always check the surf and wave conditions before starting your trip. A day-use fee of $7.50 Canadian must be paid at the park entrance. Waterfowl hunting is allowed in the marsh in the fall (September through November) on selected days of the week. Try to plan your fall trip for a day when hunters will not be in the marsh.

LAUNCH SITES:

Government Dock: A short distance south of the park gate on Rondeau Bay is a sand beach next to the government dock used for the park's boats. Washrooms and potable water and parking are

Rondeau Provincial Park

available next to the beach. It is a short carry of less than 100 feet from the parking lot to the beach.

Lake Erie Beach: East of the Visitors Centre is a public beach access site. It is a 300-foot carry from the parking lot to the water. No washrooms or potable water are available at the beach, but both are available at the Visitors Centre about 0.25 miles west of the beach.

DIRECTIONS

START: From the **government dock (N 42° 19.11' W 081° 51.00')** head south along the east shore of Rondeau Bay.

MILE 1.0: Paddling south you pass private cottages and sand beaches for the first 0.5 mile. At Mile 1.0 you reach the edge of the cattail marsh.

MILE 3.25: Continuing south you pass over shallow water and continue along the edge of the cattail marsh. At Mile 3.25 you come to a marsh channel where kayakers can head inland into the marsh at high water levels. *Caution:* At low lake levels you may not be able to enter the marsh's inland channels, and lake levels can change as much as a foot or more in a matter of a few hours due to wind or air pressure changes over Lake Erie. If you enter the marsh channels, be prepared for the possibility that the water level may drop and leave you stranded in the mud.

MILES 6.0–9.0: The cattail marsh continues for several more miles. At high water levels you can travel by the inland marsh channels. At lower water levels you will need to paddle along the edge of Rondeau Bay. As you near the harbor entrance, you pass some small marshy islands with a few trees and shrubs growing on them. At Mile 6.0 you reach the harbor entrance. *Caution:* As you leave the sheltered waters of Rondeau Bay, you may encounter rough conditions and clapotis off of the steel sheet-piling walls of the harbor entrance.

Paddling south through the harbor entrance into Lake Erie, you pass through a narrow channel with steel **sheet-piling walls (N 42° 15.35', W 081° 54.46')**. Weather permitting paddle out into Lake Erie and turn east to paddle along the sand beach shore. The Lake Erie shore is a narrow sand beach with hardwood forest just inland. At Mile 9.0 you begin to round the corner as the shore turns north. After this point you pass private cottages.

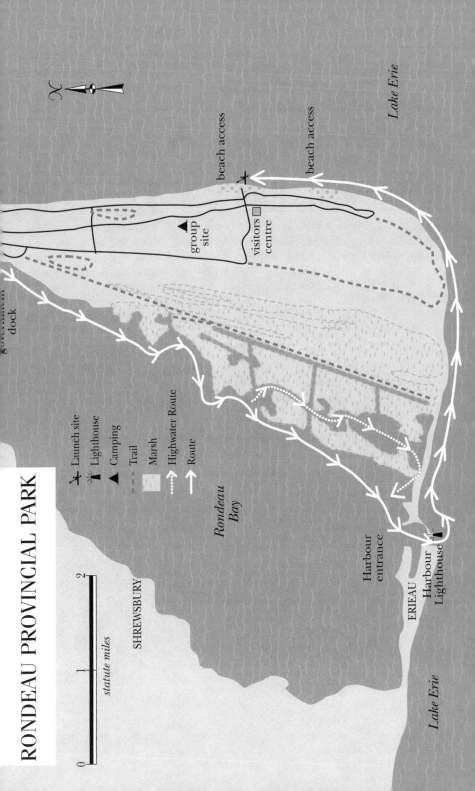

RONDEAU PROVINCIAL PARK

statute miles

0   1   2

SHREWSBURY

Rondeau
Bay

Lake Erie

ERIEAU

Harbour
entrance

Harbour
Lighthouse

government
dock

Launch site
Lighthouse
Camping
Trail
Marsh
Highwater Route
Route

group
site

visitors
centre

beach access

beach access

Lake Erie

Lake Erie

MILE 10.5: As you head north along the sand beach, you pass many private cottages. Please respect the property rights of the private landholders and do not land on these beaches except in an emergency. At Mile 10.5 there is a public beach access that is part of the park.

MILE 12.0: After passing the park beach, the narrow sand beach, and private cottages continue as you paddle north. At Mile 12.0 you come to a second park beach which is the **take-out/launch site (N 42° 16.88', W 081° 50.44')**.

Where to Eat & Where to Stay

RESTAURANTS & LODGING   For information on restaurants and lodging in the area, call the Southwestern Ontario Travel Association at (800) 661–6804. **CAMPING**   Individual sites and group campsites are available within the park. Call (519) 674–1750 for information. For information on private campgrounds in the area, call the Southwestern Ontario Travel Association (800) 661–6804.

Route 26:

▬ ▬ ▬ ▬ ▬ ▬ ▬ ▬ ▬ ▬ ▬ ▬ ➤

Long Point Provincial Park

Long Point is aptly named, a long, narrow point that extends for over 20 miles east into Lake Erie. The south side of the point consists of a typical Lake Erie sand beach shoreline, but on the north side of the peninsula, there is a huge expanse of cattail marsh. The provincial park contains only a small area of the marsh, but most of the remaining marsh has remained undeveloped as Ontario Crown land or private land maintained as a hunting reserve. The expansive marsh is ideal habitat for waterfowl and wading birds and attracts huge flocks of migratory birds.

TRIP HIGHLIGHTS: Great bird watching, exploring narrow channels and islands in a cattail marsh.

TRIP RATING:
Beginner/Intermediate: 9-mile round-trip loop through the cattail marsh channels and back.

TRIP DURATION: Day trip.

NAVIGATION AIDS: CHS chart 2110, Canadian topographical map 40 I/9 at 1:50,000.

CAUTIONS: Winds from the east can bring large seas in Sturgeon Bay, but the shallow marsh waters ensure that the main surf break is far offshore; cold water in spring and fall.

TRIP PLANNING: Pay a day-use fee of $7.50 Canadian at the park entrance. Hunting is allowed in the marsh in the fall (September through November) on selected days of the week. Try to plan your fall trip for a day when hunters will not be in the marsh. Always check the marine forecast before starting your trip. Sturgeon Bay and the cattail marsh are shallow and well sheltered, making this an ideal trip for beginning paddlers. The route map is a rough guide to the marsh channels and islands, but channels or islands will change shape or even disappear with small changes in water level. The route described may not be possible at low lake levels. Changes in wind speed and direction and air pressure can cause water levels in the Great Lakes to change by a foot or more in a matter of hours. With channel depths often just deep enough to float a kayak, it is easy to get stranded in the mud if the lake level drops. Although the marsh area within the provincial park is relatively small, it is easy to get lost in the maze of channels. Make use of the small posts with flashing light markers and marsh index posts that the park has installed for hunters. Kayakers who want to explore a larger area of the marsh should continue west of the park into Crown land marsh.

LAUNCH SITES: As you head east out on Long Point, you pass through private land and Ontario Crown land before coming to a small island of park land. Leaving the small section of park land and continuing east, you come to the main park gate. Just past the park gate, head north at the sign for the boat ramp. At the boat ramp there is parking close to the water and outhouse bathroom facilities, but no potable water.

DIRECTIONS

START: From the **park boat ramp (N 42° 35.01', W 080° 23.32')**, head north out a narrow channel lined with tall cattails and fragmites. After about 0.25 miles you enter the open water of **Sturgeon Bay**—at the mouth of this small channel is a post with a flashing light marker. Take note of the marker so you will recognize the channel on your return to the boat ramp. To the south and east of the channel marker is a waterfowl feeding area. Boats (yes, that means kayakers, too) are not allowed there to ensure that birds can feed undisturbed.

MILE 1.0: Heading northwest along the edge of the cattail marsh, you come to the flashing light marker post D. Turn southwest, entering the narrow channel between the islands of cattails.

MILE 2.0: Passing through the long, narrow channel between the cattail-covered islands, you enter a wider channel area near the flashing light

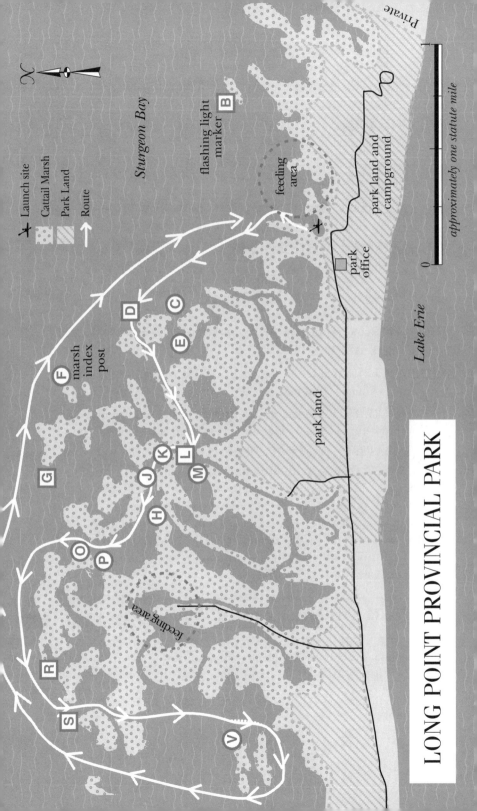

LONG POINT PROVINCIAL PARK

approximately one statute mile

0

Lake Erie

Sturgeon Bay

Private

Launch site
Cattail Marsh
Park Land
Route

flashing light marker

feeding area

park office

park land and campground

park land

marsh index post

feeding area

B

D
C
E
F
G

K
L
M
J
H
O
P

R
S
V

marker post L. At marker L, head north through the narrow channel past markers K, J, and H.

MILE 2.5: Past marker H, the channel widens. Continue north past markers P and O and exit into the open waters of Sturgeon Bay.

MILE 3.25: Heading west along the edge of the marsh, you pass islands covered with tall cattails. Continue past the flashing marker post R. At the flashing marker post S, turn south.

MILE 4.25: Passing south through a narrow channel between islands, you enter a larger open bay and continue south past marker post V. Past marker V, round the small cattail-covered islands. Return north along the outside edge of the cattail marsh and the open waters of Sturgeon Bay, then east to the boat ramp launch site. Paddlers who want to explore more of the marsh can continue west into the area of the marsh that is Crown land.

Where to Eat & Where to Stay

RESTAURANTS & LODGING For information on restaurants in the area, call the Southwestern Ontario Travel Association at (800) 661–6804. **CAMPING** Individual and group campsites are available within the park. Call (519) 674–1750 for information. For information on private campgrounds in the area, call the Southwestern Ontario Travel Association (800) 661–6804.

Lake Ontario & the St. Lawrence River

Ontario

Route 27:

Niagara River

This route follows a section of the Niagara River from the river's mouth on Lake Ontario south toward the Niagara Gorge and Falls (but not too close!). The river flows through the high wooded bluffs of the Niagara Escarpment out to the sandy shores of Lake Ontario. This is not only a good paddle, but also a great area to visit for many other reasons. Besides the Falls there are the two forts (Old Fort Niagara and Fort George), the Shaw Festival, and a number of good vineyards on the Ontario side. This is also a good place for bird-watchers to look for a variety of gulls (unfortunately, the best gull watching is in December, making for some cold paddling).

TRIP HIGHLIGHTS: Good scenery, historic area.

TRIP RATING:
Intermediate: 10–12-mile trip from the mouth of the river upstream and back.

TRIP DURATION: Full day.

NAVIGATION AIDS: Canadian topographic map: *Niagara Falls* (30 M/3, 6); CHS chart 14816; USGS: *Lewiston and Old Fort Niagara* at 1:24,000 or *Niagara County* at 1:50,000.

CAUTIONS: Boat traffic, strong currents, and potential for standing waves at the river's mouth if Lake Ontario is rough; currents may be strong at high water and downstream of Lewiston.

TRIP PLANNING: This paddle starts at the mouth of the river either at Fort Niagara on the New York side or at Niagara-on-the-Lake on the Ontario side, and goes upstream to near Lewiston, where the river channel constricts suddenly and the rapids begin.

Unless you want a workout, you should avoid paddling the river in the spring when the water is high and the current faster. You may want to turn around prior to Lewiston if the current is too much. Whichever side of the river you launch from, be sure to get an early start. Parking close to the water may be in short supply later in the day. Although you will not be exposed to wind and waves from the open lake, strong winds can funnel down the valley, and if they are blowing against the current, you can expect things to get pretty choppy. This is a pleasant area to visit in the spring and fall when the crowds are smaller, but the weather is still mild.

LAUNCH SITE: To get to the put-in at Niagara-on-the-Lake, take Queen Elizabeth Way (QEW) to Highway 55 and drive north on 55 for 7 miles until it ends at Queen Street. Turn east on Queen Street and drive 0.5 mile to the intersection of Queen and King Streets. Go left/north on King for 0.7 mile, then turn left onto Front/Ricardo Street and the waterfront park with the gazebo and a riverside beach just down the hill. The park has public rest rooms, but most of the parking is metered or in the self-pay lot so bring some change. There are boat ramps across the river at Fort Niagara State Park; however, there is an entrance fee for the park and a launch fee at the ramp, and the ramps are the steep, concrete variety.

START: From the **beach** at Niagara-on-the-Lake, paddle southeast upriver. The impressive ramparts of **Old Fort Niagara** are just across the river on the eastern shore, and if the air is clear, you can see the skyscrapers of Toronto across the lake to the north. Paddle past the marina and docks on the west shore and follow the shore as it turns almost due south.

MILE 0.5: Near the bend in the river, you will begin to see **Fort George**. From the river it will be difficult to see much more than the earthworks and stockade surrounding the fort. The **Old Navy Hall** is the only structure located on the waterfront; look for a smallish stone building. Opposite Fort George, on the east side of the river, is **Fort Niagara State Park** and then the buildings of **Youngstown**.

MILES 1.0–5.5: After Fort George the land rises to form high bluffs on the Canadian side. At low water, however, there are occasional small gravel beaches at the base of the bluffs, where it's possible to land. The bluffs are not quite as high on the American side, but the land has many more houses and cottages. The Canadian shore has a parkway and bike trail that runs along the top of the bluffs and some private homes. Near **Lewiston** the current picks up. Turn around and head back when the current gets to be too much or when you get tired of paddling upstream. Paddle back the way you came to the put-in.

Where to Eat & Where to Stay

RESTAURANTS & LODGING Due to the attractions of Niagara Falls and the Shaw Festival in Niagara-on-the-Lake, accommodations are expensive, particularly for the latter, during which most lodging will be in the $100/night and up range. Less expensive motels can be found in Niagara Falls for those who can stand the tourist hype and crowds. For information on lodging and dining (and wineries and theater) in Niagara-on-the-Lake, call the Chamber of Commerce at (905) 468–4263, or call the Niagara and Mid-Western Ontario Travel Association at (800) 267–3399 for information about the greater Niagara region (Ontario side). For information about the New York side of the river, call the Niagara County Tourism Department at (800) 338–7890. **CAMPING** The best camping is found on the New York side at the state parks. **Four-Mile Creek State Park** is a short distance from Old Fort Niagara: Call (716) 745–7611 for information. **Hamlin** Beach is farther away, but still on the Lake Ontario Parkway. Call (716) 964–2462 for more information.

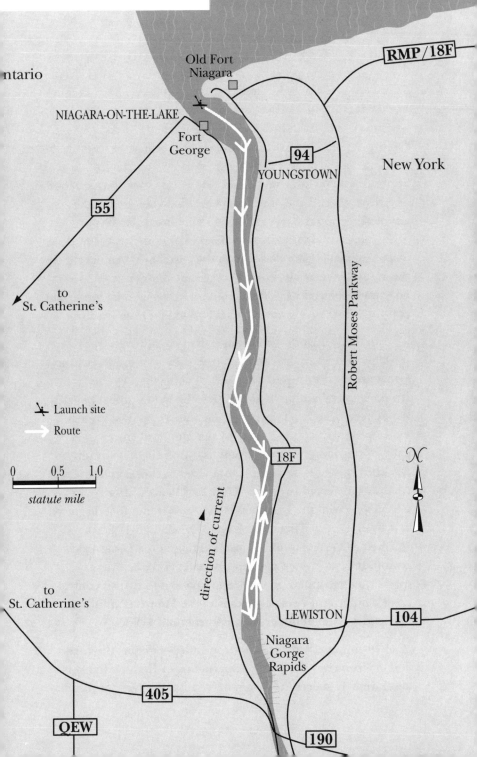

NIAGARA RIVER

Lake Ontario

Ontario

Old Fort
Niagara

NIAGARA-ON-THE-LAKE

Fort
George

RMP/18F

94

YOUNGSTOWN

New York

55

to
St. Catherine's

Robert Moses Parkway

⤞ Launch site

⟹ Route

0   0.5   1.0
statute mile

18F

direction of current

to
St. Catherine's

LEWISTON

104

Niagara
Gorge
Rapids

405

QEW

190

Old Fort Niagara & Fort George

There are few places in the Great Lakes region where so much history is concentrated in such a small area. The Niagara River was important to all the successive inhabitants of the area (Native, French, British, and American) because of its critical location. At the Niagara River the outflow from Lakes Superior, Michigan, Huron, and Erie is funneled through the one river, which flows into Lake Ontario. The Great Lakes and their tributaries were used as waterways by the Native Americans and then early European explorers and fur traders when exchanging goods between the eastern settlements and the vast interior of the North American continent. The Niagara River and its portage routes represented an important control point, having commercial and military significance.

Initially, the only way around the Niagara Falls was by portage, and when the French began their exploration of the Great Lakes, they found this portage controlled by the Iroquois (a federation of five tribes, the westernmost being the Seneca, who lived near the Niagara River). The French made several attempts to occupy the mouth of the river in spite of hostilities with the Iroquois, who were allied with the British. Eventually, the French obtained permission to build what they referred to as the "House of Peace" after negotiating with the Iroquois. It was, however, a fort disguised as a trading post. This is the "castle" of Old Fort Niagara, finished in 1726, and the oldest building in the Great Lakes region. It does indeed resemble a castle and has a very medieval atmosphere. Fort Niagara passed to British control after a bitter, two-week siege during the French and Indian War and remained under their control until 1796.

During the War for American Independence, the fort and environs was the base of operations of Butler's Rangers, an extremely successful group of loyalist refugees responsible for devastating attacks against settlers and rebel forces. Fort Niagara was eventually transferred to the Americans following the end of the war. The British then began constructing Fort George on the west bank of the river to protect the new border and the area to the west, now home to many loyalist refugees who fled the thirteen colonies for Canada.

Following a brief period of peace in the Niagara region, both Fort Niagara and Fort George were involved in the War of 1812. There were several exchanges of artillery fire, during which Fort George held the advantage, being located on higher ground. Initially, Fort George fell to the Americans following an attack by a naval squadron, but the Americans withdrew after leveling the fort and destroying the nearby town, then called Newark. The British not only reoccupied Fort George, but also captured Fort Niagara and burned nearby Youngstown. Fort Niagara was held by the British until the end of the war in 1814 when it was returned to the Americans under the terms of the Treaty of Ghent. Both forts were not only maintained after the war, but the defenses were improved in preparation for further conflict. The fortifications were abandoned after the construction of the Erie Canal in 1825 made the Niagara portage essentially irrelevant.

Both Fort George and Old Fort Niagara have been restored and feature park interpreters in period costume and many good exhibits on the history of the forts and the War of 1812. They are best visited by land and not by kayak, and shouldn't be missed if you have an interest in the history of the area. Admission fees apply for both forts. For information on Old Fort Niagara, call (716) 745–7611; for information about Fort George, call (905) 468–7687.

Route 28:

━ ━ ━ ━ ━ ━ ━ ━ ━ ━ ━ ━ ━ ━ ━ ━ ━ ➤

Toronto: Humber River

The Humber River paddle starts on the Toronto waterfront, offering good views of downtown, and then wanders north up the river. A quick look at a map of the area will show that the river is lined with parks or other green spaces for most of its length, and while this is definitely an urban paddle, it's a relatively relaxing and pleasant trip.

TRIP HIGHLIGHTS: Good scenery, peaceful urban paddle.

TRIP RATING:

Beginner: 4–8 mile paddle from Sunnyside Beach up the Humber River and back (inside barrier walls).

Intermediate: In addition to the Beginner route, practice braces in clapotis along the outside of barrier walls.

TRIP DURATION: Part to full day.

NAVIGATION AIDS: Canadian topographic map 30 M/11 at 1:50,000 or any detailed city map.

CAUTIONS: Some boat traffic, reflection waves at barrier walls along waterfront.

TRIP PLANNING: This leisurely paddle doesn't require too much preparation, and your biggest challenge may be avoiding the crowds at the launch area. Paddling weekdays shouldn't be too much of a problem, but if you are paddling on a summer weekend, try to get to the park early as the parking lots along the water are not huge. The cement barrier walls lining the western beaches allow easy launches even on a rough day, the only tricky spot being the river mouth itself.

LAUNCH SITE: Take the QEW or Gardiner Expressway to Park Lawn Road. Go south on Park Lawn to Lakeshore Boulevard, then east on Sunnyside Beach. The beach is about a 100-yard carry from the lot. If it is too crowded in the lot, get back on Lakeshore Boulevard going west. Turn left at Park Lawn Road into Humber Park East, which has several lots. The only disadvantage to this spot is the short section between the launch and the river (there are no barrier walls here). There is no charge for parking, and the parks do have restrooms.

DIRECTIONS

START: From the **Sunnyside Park** beach, paddle west. There is a wall made of cement sections with periodic gaps that runs along the western beaches. You have a choice of paddling in the sheltered area next to shore or on the outside of the walls. *Caution:* Like any flat and near-vertical surface, this wall is very good at generating clapotis. It can be fun to play in if you're ready for it, and a good place to practice bracing. If you're just looking for a quiet paddle on windy days stay on the inside.

MILES 0.5–1.0: At the mouth of the **Humber River** is the arch of the **Humber Bay Bike Bridge.** Turn right and paddle north under the bridge. *Caution:* Watch for small motorboats passing in and out of the river mouth. If it is rough out on the lake, this may be a difficult spot, particularly if there is any current from the river. Use caution before proceeding.

Next you get to paddle beneath four bridges and about twenty-five lanes of traffic. This is the least pleasant part of the paddle, but keep paddling. After you emerge from the dark underbelly of the overpasses, you will find a marshy area. Keep well away from the banks of the river in this section: Low water revealed a great deal of kayak-eating debris (twisted rebar, jagged cement, glass, etc.) that would otherwise be hidden in the muddy water.

MILE 1.5: After the marshes the river winds between wooded bluffs—a very pleasant section.

MILE 2.0: There is a boat launching area on the west side of the river, then the docks of the **Humber Valley Yacht Club**. If you're lucky you may

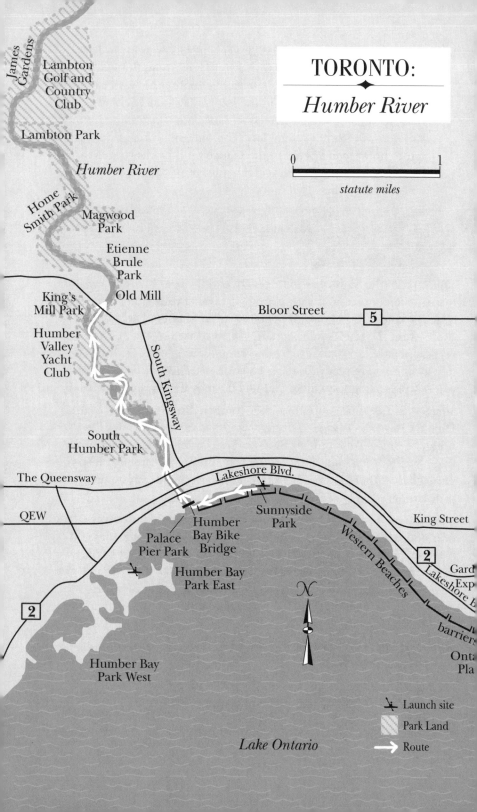

find dragon boats moored there. When the boats are not racing, the dragon heads are not mounted on the prows, but you can't miss the brightly painted boats. Continue paddling upstream as far as you want or as far as current and water depth allows. North of **Bloor Street** the river narrows and several small islands divide the river into narrow channels around Old Mill. North of the **Old Mill** area are several golf courses and more small parks along the river.

MILES 2.0–4.0: Paddle back down the river, out to the lake, and back to your launch point.

Where to Eat & Where to Stay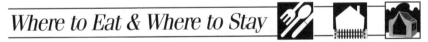

RESTAURANTS & LODGING No shortage here. Call Tourism Toronto (416–203–2500) for a list of accommodations and restaurants. If you are not on a budget, then there are any number of places to stay. Good motels may take a little time to find, but there are several all in a row just east of the entrance to East Humber Bay Park on Lakeshore Boulevard. Be warned, however, that some rent rooms by the hour, while others are still providing rooms for out-of-town visitors. Try the **Inn on the Lake** at (416) 766–4392. **CAMPING** Not too many choices here, but what did you expect! Still the **Indian Line Campground** is not bad; they are located on Indian Line Road near the northern city limits. Call (416) 661–6600 for more information. **Darlington Provincial Park** is located about an hour's drive east of downtown Toronto. Call (905) 436–2036 for information or reservations.

Route 29:

━ ▬ ▬ ━ ▬ ▬ ▬ ▬ ▬ ▬ ━ ▬ ━ ▬ ⟶

Toronto Islands

This archipelago is just 1 mile south of Toronto and makes a great day paddle destination, with opportunities for sidetrips to quiet little bays or paddling the Inner Harbour, which offers an excellent view of the Toronto skyline. The islands were once a peninsula formed by sediment deposited at the mouth of the Don River, but a storm in 1858 washed away part of the peninsula and created the Eastern Gap. The islands are government owned, but land on Ward's and Algonquin Islands is leased to residents. There is also an airport on the western end of the island (Hanlan's Point), an amusement park on Centre Island, and numerous marinas, including that of the Royal Canadian Yacht Club. The island group has regular ferry service, but paddlers only have to cross the Eastern Gap from Cherry Beach to get to the islands.

TRIP HIGHLIGHTS: Good views, good scenery.

TRIP RATING:
   Beginner: 7.0-mile paddle from Cherry Beach around the Inner Harbour islands and back.
   Intermediate: Add one or more sidetrips for a total distance of 8–17 miles.

TRIP DURATION: Part to full day.

NAVIGATION AIDS: Canadian topographic map 30 M/11 or any detailed street map of downtown Toronto.

CAUTIONS: Boat traffic, some exposure to wind and waves off the open lake.

TRIP PLANNING: This is a relatively sheltered paddle, but there is one open section between Cherry Beach and the Eastern Gap, so it wouldn't hurt to check the marine forecast before setting out. Ferries run out to the islands frequently during the summer, bringing plenty of visitors to the islands and Centre Island Park. If you are looking to avoid crowds and boat traffic, you can try avoiding the weekends or paddle during spring or fall. Lake Ontario remains largely ice free during the winter, but if you paddle then, be sure to wear a wet suit or dry suit! Local paddlers recommended staying away from the Western Gap entrance to the Inner Harbour, where most of the commercial shipping traffic enters the harbor.

LAUNCH SITE: From Lakeshore Boulevard East, take Cherry Street south to the end of the road at Cherry Beach. There is a series of lots along the beach with no charge to park. There are restrooms at the beach although they were closed the day we launched. It is only a 25–50-yard carry from the lots to the water.

DIRECTIONS

START: Paddle southwest from **Cherry Beach** toward the Eastern Gap.

MILE 0.5: Turn north and paddle into the **Eastern Gap**. *Caution:* Keep an eye out for small- and medium-sized craft as you paddle through the gap. If traffic is heavy, it could get fairly choppy in here. Once you reach the end of the breakwater, turn and paddle southwest past Ward's Island toward Algonquin Island (Ward's Island is not actually an island, but part of the Toronto Island).

MILE 1.0: Turn and paddle southwest through the channel between **Ward's** and **Algonquin Islands**. This stretch resembles a canal, with small bridges arching over the water from **Toronto Island** to the smaller islands. The south side of the waterway is lined by a vertical stone wall, and although you could use the ladders provided for moored boats, this is not a great place for kayaks to land. You should see plenty of ducks, geese, and swans here. Continue paddling southwest.

MILES 1.0–2.0: Look for the docks belonging to the Royal Canadian Yacht Club around **South Island**.

Toronto Islands

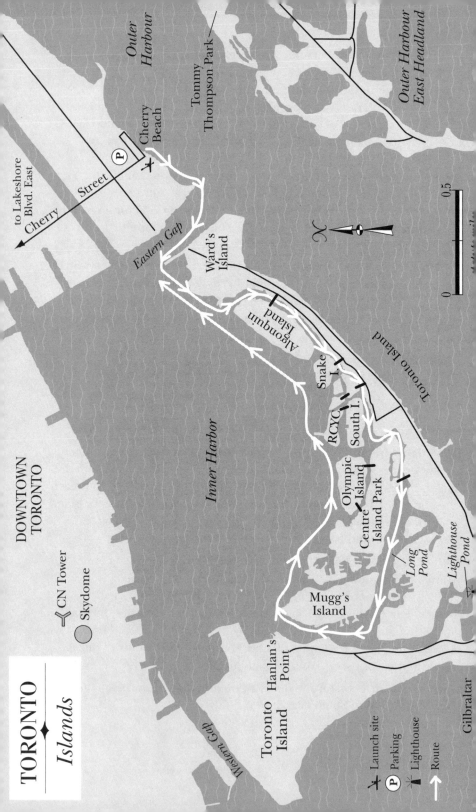

MILE 2.5: Paddle around the eastern end of **Centre Island**. This is one of its busiest sections because of the amusement park. As you head northwest, the narrow channel opens up into the **Long Pond**. *Caution:* You will see lots of docks along the west ends of Center and Mugg's Islands, so watch out for boat traffic along this stretch.

MILE 3.25: Turn and paddle north along the western shore of **Mugg's Island**. Apart from all the docks, there is a bird sanctuary on this island. *Sidetrip:* From the western end of Long Pond, paddle south to visit Lighthouse Pond, where you'll find the old lighthouse, now rather overgrown. This will add only about 1.0 mile to your trip. At the end of

Toronto Islands

the eighteenth century, this area was the center for British military operations until the fortifications on the islands were destroyed by the Americans during the War of 1812.

MILE 3.75: When you reach the northern end of Mugg's Island, turn and paddle east. To the north is **Hanlan's Point**, where the Toronto Island Airport is located. *Caution:* As you paddle this section, be aware of the ferries that run from the mainland to Hanlan's Point and Center and Ward's Islands, as well as the numerous small motorboats in the area.

MILES 4.0–5.5: Paddle along the arc of islands as it curves to the north. **Olympic Island** has snack bars and a swimming beach.

MILES 5.5–7.0: Paddle around the breakwall and back into the Eastern Gap, returning to Cherry Beach. *Sidetrip:* If the lake is calm, you can extend your paddle by paddling along the southern beaches of Toronto Island. Total distance from Cherry Beach to Gibraltar Point and back is about 6.0 miles. For a quieter paddle or addition to the Toronto Islands trip, cross southeast to the Outer Harbour East Headland and explore the bays and marshes around Tommy Thompson Park. The total distance will be about 2.0 to 3.0 miles, including a 0.5-mile crossing from Cherry Beach and back. Watch out for boat traffic when crossing.

Where to Eat & Where to Stay

RESTAURANTS, LODGINGS & CAMPING
See Route 28: Toronto: Humber River.

Route 30:

---------------------------→

Presqu'ile Provincial Park

This area is another section of limestone shoreline like that seen on the Bruce Peninsula and elsewhere around the Great Lakes. The park is located on a tombolo (an island that has become linked to the mainland by a sand- or gravel bar). The northern leg of the park consists of a sandbar with a long beach on one side and marshes on the other. The park is known as one of the best birding places in Ontario. Like other peninsulas around the Great Lakes, it acts as a collector for migrating birds, and the marshes on the east side attract a lot of migrating waterfowl. More than 320 species of birds have been seen within the park, and more than 120 nest there. There is also a (nonoperating) lighthouse in the park and a variety of landscapes: open fields, marshes, sand dunes, and the cedar forest that grows on the limestone rock found on the south side of the peninsula.

TRIP HIGHLIGHTS: Good scenery, lighthouse, good bird watching.

TRIP RATING:
Beginner: 5-mile trip from Calf Pasture Point to Presqu'ile Point and back, or a 4-mile trip to the marshes and back.
Intermediate: 16-mile paddle from Calf Pasture Point to Owen Point and back.

TRIP DURATION: Part to full day.

NAVIGATION AIDS: Canadian topographic maps: *Trenton* (31C/H) or 30 N/13 at 1:50,000. Alternatively you can probably get by with the park map.

CAUTIONS: Exposure to west and south winds and motorboat traffic; currents may be present near Presqu'ile and Owen Points.

TRIP PLANNING: If bird watching is your goal, you will need to decide what you would most like to see: Waterfowl start arriving in February and March, songbirds in April. The gulls, cormorants, terns, and herons that nest on the islands instead of passing through will be around for the summer. Although ice is less of a problem on the eastern Great Lakes, March and April are definitely wet suit/dry suit months. The park offers a number of birding activities—from workshops to periodic bird counts and waterfowl viewing festivals. Contact the park office at (613) 475–4324 for more information. The park has several hundred campsites for those who want to overnight at the park and is the only provincial park in the area to be open for camping year- round. Due to shoals and the rock shoreline around the southern side of the peninsula and the potential for currents around Owen and Presqu'ile Points, this would be a poor choice for a rough-weather paddle. We experienced some rather strong currents (for the Great Lakes, anyway) around Gull and High Bluff Islands in only moderate winds. Check the marine forecast before starting your paddle.

LAUNCH SITE: From Highway 401, take Highway 30 south to Brighton, then take Highway 2 west from the center of town. The turnoff for the park road is only a few blocks from the Highway 2/30 intersection and is marked with a provincial park sign. Turn south onto the park road and follow it through a residential neighborhood to the park gate. You will need to stop at the gate and get a permit; pick up a park map while you are there. Continue down the park road to the Calf Pasture turnoff and drive east to the end of the road. There is a picnic area with outhouses and a boat launching area. You could also launch from any of the cobble beaches along the south side of the peninsula, but these beaches are difficult to deal with in any kind of surf. The beaches can be steep in some areas, and the lake bottom close to shore is a flat rock shelf, not the place to land in rough weather.

DIRECTIONS

START: Put in at Calf Pasture and paddle southeast along the shore. The land between **Calf Pasture Point** and **Presqu'ile Point** is private and lined with residential homes. *Sidetrip:* If you're looking for waterfowl or a

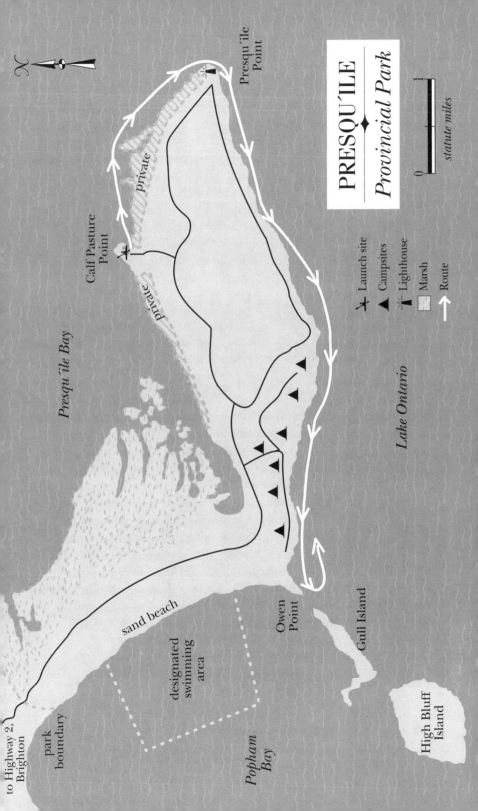

PRESQU'ILE
Provincial Park

statute miles

✕ Launch site
▲ Campsites
✴ Lighthouse
▨ Marsh
⬆ Route

to Highway 2,
Brighton

park
boundary

sand beach

designated
swimming
area

Popham
Bay

Owen
Point

Gull Island

High Bluff
Island

Presqu'ile Bay

Calf Pasture
Point

Private

Private

Presqu'ile
Point

Lake Ontario

short and quiet paddle, take a tour of the marshes by paddling west along the shore until you reach the grassy areas. The total distance to the marshes and back to Calf Pasture Point is about 4.0 miles.

MILE 2.5: The park land starts just before Presqu'ile Point. Look for the white, eight-sided lighthouse at the point. The original glass cupola is gone, leaving the tower with a flat top. There is a visitor center there, and if the seas are calm around the point, you can land on the cobble beach and get out for a look around. Those who are just visiting the lighthouse should paddle back to Calf Pasture Point by the same route. Others should continue around the point and paddle west along the south side of the peninsula. *Caution:* Wait for calm weather before paddling the next part of the route. Most of the shoreline offers poor landing in anything but flat water, and strong winds can cause currents around Presqu'ile and Owen Points.

MILES 2.5–5.5: There is a park road running along the shore with group camping and day-use/picnic areas.

MILES 5.5–8.0: Turn and follow the shoreline as it curves a little to the north. The **campgrounds** are located along this section of shore. The beaches are gravel to cobble and can be used for a break in calm weather.

MILE 8.5: At **Owen Point** you have choice of turning around and going back the way you came, or you can continue north to visit the sand beaches before you return (but please don't paddle in the swimming area). *Sidetrip:* High Bluff and Gull Islands are off limits during nesting season (March 10–September 30), but if you are paddling after nesting season, you can include a circuit of the islands. There seem to be blinds set up on the island, probably for observing birds. A good variety nest on the island, including ring-billed gulls, double-breasted cormorants, herring gulls, terns, and even black-crowned night herons. If the birds are nesting, please don't disturb them by getting too close—bring a pair of binoculars and view them from a distance. In the early nineteenth century, the *Speedy* was lost off High Bluff Island, with no survivors. There are extensive shoals around the island, so stay well away from the shore in any kind of rough weather.

Where to Eat & Where to Stay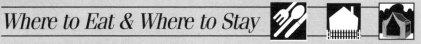

RESTAURANTS & LODGING For a list of accommodations and restaurants in the Brighton area, contact the Bay of Quinte Tourist Council at (613) 962–4597. **CAMPING** There are almost 400 sites within the park, but reservations are recommended during the summer. To make a reservation, call the park at (613) 475–2204.

Lake Ontario & the St. Lawrence River

The Thousand Islands

The Thousand Islands

The 50-mile stretch of the St. Lawrence from Kingston to Brockville is aptly called the Thousand Islands. The area, with its lovely scenery—hundreds of small granite islands covered by oak and pine forests—is just gaining a reputation as a kayaking destination. There are many private homes and cottages on the islands. Scattered throughout, however, are islands belonging to one of several park systems, with beaches, picnic areas, trails, and campsites for visitors to use.

The islands are busy during the summer, but they are great for off-season paddling. The windier fall weather doesn't do more than kick up a little chop, even though a few miles away there may be 6-foot waves on Lake Ontario. Except at high water there is noticeable current in only a few places, making it easy to paddle upstream as well as down. The river begins to freeze up at the end of October, and ice-out occurs in April. If you are doing spring or fall paddling, a wet suit or dry suit is definitely recommended, but the water is quite warm in the summer.

One challenge is the sometimes very heavy boat traffic. The worst of it, including some very big ships, is found in the American Channel along the south shore of the river. One local kayaker described this channel as a "slaughter bin" at peak season, and it is best just to stay the heck out of the way. If you must paddle near or across the shipping lane, use extreme caution. The bigger ships have very little maneuvering room in the narrow channel and cannot stop quickly. Partly for this reason, most of the routes described in the following section leave from the Canadian side of the river where the boat traffic is somewhat lighter, and there are no big ships (except for the tour boats).

The U.S.-Canadian border runs through the middle of the river; carry a map that shows its exact location. The presence of the border can cause complications due to customs regulations: The rules state that if you start on one side but visit any island across the border, you must check in with customs when you return. The only route described here that is problematic is Boldt Castle, which does have its own customs station on Heart Island. (All others start and remain on one side of the border.) Canadian citizens visiting the island must bring a passport. U.S.

citizens are spared this rigmarole if they leave from the American side, but must cross the shipping lane to reach Heart Island.

Island camping is available mainly within the St. Lawrence Islands National Park. Campsites are available on a first come, first served basis. Although the docks may be crowded, many boaters stay on their boats rather than in the tent sites. The park is also adding some canoe/kayak-only sites over the next few years, so check with the park office for an update on these sites. If you use a dock to land and unload (and you will have to on some islands), you owe a docking fee in addition to the camping fee; both are paid at fee boxes on the islands. The park is fully operational between Victoria Day and (Canadian) Thanksgiving, but open to camping year round (camping and docking are free during the off-season).

A number of New York State Parks exist along the St. Lawrence. Most have car access and are crowded during the summer season, but the mainland parks make good places to launch from because they all have ramps or docks for boaters.

For the state parks, reservations are not only available but highly recommended (the St. Lawrence parks are very busy during the summer). There are fewer island campsites on the American side; but Cedar Island, Mary Island, and Canoe Point all have camping and no road access. Call and ask for the *Island Parks* and *Thousand Islands State Park Region* brochures that have maps of the campsites and campground capacities.

The only provincial park with camping in this area is Ivy Lea, which has a campground on the mainland not far from the Thousand Islands International Bridge. It also has a boat launching area and can be used as a point to start day trips as well. Call (800) 437–2233 for information.

Contact Numbers for Parks in the Thousand Islands

St. Lawrence Islands National Park (Canada): (613) 923–5261

Parks of the St. Lawrence (Ontario Provincial Parks): (800) 437–2233

New York State Parks (Thousand Islands Regional Office): (315) 482–2593

New York State Park Campsite Reservations: (800) 456–2267

Route 31:

━━ ━━ ━━ ━━ ━━ ━━ ━━ ━━ ━━ ━━ ━━ ━━ ▶

Kingston to Cedar Island

This simple and short day paddle is especially fine in the morning or evening when the light hits the walls and towers of Fort Henry on the hill across the water from Cedar Island. The island, part of the St. Lawrence Islands National Park, has picnic areas, short trails, and even camping available. The paddle also starts out on the Cataraqui River, which is part of the Rideau Canal System, leading from Kingston to Ottawa. Fort Henry guards the entrance to the Rideau Canal, and old guard towers line the Kingston waterfront, a legacy of the War of 1812. Cedar Island has one of these round towers on its western end, a short walk away from the docks.

TRIP HIGHLIGHTS: Good views of Fort Henry and Kingston, trails to old tower.

TRIP RATING:
    Beginner: 7-mile trip from the Cataraqui River in Kingston around Cedar Island and back.

TRIP DURATION: Part to full day.

NAVIGATION AIDS: Canadian topographic maps 31 C/1, 31 C/8, NOAA chart 14768.

CAUTIONS: Boat traffic, some exposure to wind and waves on crossing to Cedar Island.

TRIP PLANNING: The island is popular with boaters out for a picnic. If you want a quieter visit, try a weekday or an off-season paddle (before Victoria Day, after Canadian Thanksgiving). If you want to try camping on the island, the same advice applies.

Campsites are first come, first served, and although other boaters tend to stay on their boats rather than set up a tent, there is no guarantee that there will be a site waiting for you. If you will be camping during a peak season weekend, try to nab a site early in the day just to be sure. (See the section introduction for docking and camping fees and rules.)

LAUNCH SITE: Launch from the public ramp located next to the old Woolen Mill and the Cataraqui Canoe Club building. Get on King Street/Highway 2 through downtown Kingston. Two blocks west of the bridge over the Cataraqui River, turn west onto Barrack Street for two blocks, then turn north onto Rideau Street. Continue north for seven blocks, then turn east onto Cataraqui Street and drive two blocks to the end of the road at the Historic Woolen Mill. There is a public boat launch and parking lot (no charge to use either). This is a sheltered spot, and there is not much current in the river.

START: Paddle south from the boat ramp on the Cataraqui River toward the Highway 2 bridge. *Caution:* Watch for motorboat traffic when paddling under the bridge.

MILE 1.0: After the bridge you will see the **Wolfe Island Ferry** dock on the west side of the riverbank: Be sure to stay well away from it as the ferries arrive and depart frequently and move very quickly. Along the eastern bank of the river is a stone wall with fairly shallow water: a good place for clapotis if boat wakes or waves from the lake are of any size.

MILE 1.5: At this point you will want to check the lake before leaving the Cataraqui River because the 1.0 mile crossing out to **Cedar Island** is exposed to wind and waves from the southwest. Turn to the southeast and paddle to the western end of the island. The Royal Military College is located next to **Navy Bay**.

MILE 2.5: Turn and paddle to the northeast, following the shore of Cedar Island.

MILE 3.5: There are two sets of docks on the island: one in a small bay just before the northeast end of the island, and one at the tip. Both are fairly sheltered, and the small bay also has a tiny area where it may be possible to pull a boat or two up on the weeds. Otherwise the island is fairly rocky (it is composed mainly of very old limestone); good kayak landing spots are difficult to find. There is a trail that loops around the camping and picnic areas and ends up at the southwest end of the island where the tower is. This is the **Cathcart Redoubt**, built in 1847 when **Fort Henry** was rebuilt during the Oregon Crisis, a period of tension between the U.S. and Canada. There is a good view of Fort Henry from the hill. After you reach the tip of the island, turn and paddle to the southwest. This side of the island is pretty rocky too, and landing will be difficult in anything but total calm. There is a picnic area about halfway down the island, but it's better to park at the docks and walk to the shelter.

MILE 4.0: When you reach the southwestern tip of the island, turn and paddle west toward the mouth of the Cataraqui River.

MILES 4.0–7.0: Return to the starting point by the same route.

Kingston to Cedar Island

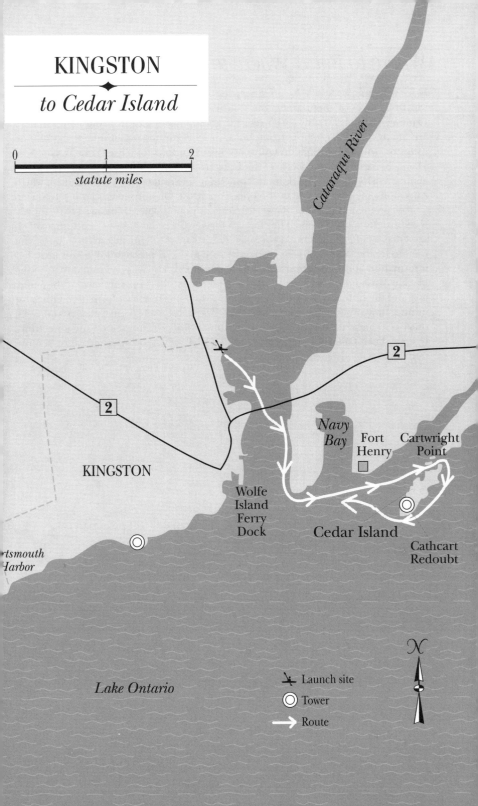

KINGSTON
to Cedar Island

0   1   2

statute miles

Cataraqui River

2

2

KINGSTON

Navy Bay

Fort Henry

Cartwright Point

Wolfe Island Ferry Dock

Cedar Island

Cathcart Redoubt

tsmouth Iarbor

Lake Ontario

✈ Launch site

◎ Tower

→ Route

N

Where to Eat & Where to Stay

RESTAURANTS Plenty of 'em here, and some pretty good ones. You will find many of them along the downtown section of Princess Street. Try the **Laundry Café** at 291 Princess Street for good, informal dining and coffee. There are many others, ranging from pubs to fine dining establishments. Call the Kingston Tourist Information Office at (888) 855–4555 for a list. **LODGING** Many choices here, too: Contact the Information Office for a list. There are several inexpensive motels on Highway 2 on either side of town and on Route 15, which runs along the eastern side of the Cataraqui River. One unusual option is to stay in a cabin on the musem ship, *Alexander Henry*, now permanently moored at the downtown Kingston Waterfront. The ship is a former Canadian Coast Guard ship, which served as a light tender and icebreaker. Cabins are authentically spartan, but if you want to try the fancier officers' cabins be sure to make a reservation in advance. For information and reservations, call (613) 542–0043. The ship is located next to the Marine Museum of the Great Lakes, which has exhibits on shipwrecks, shipbuilding, and the history of Great Lakes shipping. Call the Tourist Information Office for information about the museum. **CAMPING** Aside from Cedar Island itself, there is a campground just east of Kingston on Route 2, located on the waterfront. Call the **Lake Ontario Campground** at (613) 542–6574 for information or reservations.

Route 32:

Gananoque to the Admiralty Islands

he Admiralty Island group is located just off shore from Gananoque and makes a good choice for a leisurely paddle and picnic. Camping is also available on several of the islands for those who want an overnight trip. These islands are so close together that it doesn't take long to get a lot of island-hopping done. McDonald Island even has a real sand beach, a rarity in the islands (but watch out for poison ivy in the sandy areas). Many of the islands of the St. Lawrence were named by a British navy officer and commemorate people and ships of the War of 1812. The Admiralty group is named after other naval officers and lords of the admiralty.

TRIP HIGHLIGHTS: Picnicking, camping, sand beach.

TRIP RATING:
> *Beginner:* 7-mile trip (minimum distance) around the island group.
> *Intermediate:* Add a trip to the Lake Fleet Islands (see Rte. 33).

TRIP DURATION: Part day to overnight.

NAVIGATION AIDS: Canadian topographic map: *Gananoque* 31C/8 at 1:50,000, NOAA chart 14767.

CAUTIONS: Motorboat and tour boat traffic.

TRIP PLANNING: This is a busy area, with many private residences, tour boats, and marinas. If you are looking for a little peace and quiet, try an off-season trip. Don't let the traffic put you off: These islands are certainly worth seeing, particularly the outer islands like Aubrey and Mermaid Islands. If you want to try camping, have a second choice in mind if the campground at your first destination is full. (See the section introduction for more information on island camping.) With the exception of McDonald, these islands are fairly steep and rocky, and you should plan on using the docks to land and unload.

LAUNCH SITE: Take Highway 2 to Gananoque. Turn south on Main Street (it runs north–south and is located one block west of the bridge over the Gananoque River) and drive south to the next intersection. Turn right/west onto Clarence Street. Drive two blocks, then turn right/north onto Bay Road. The Municipal Marina is at the junction of Clarence Street and Bay Road; this is where you will park if you are staying out overnight. From the intersection and marina, drive 0.2 mile on Bay Road to the Rotary Beach on the left and small parking lot on the right. If you are going out overnight, you will have to unload your gear at the beach, then drive around the block (Bay Road is one way) and park at the marina. Launching and parking at the beach is free, but there is a charge to park at the marina. There are no toilets at the beach; try the marina instead.

DIRECTIONS

START: From the beach in **Gananoque**, paddle south toward McDonald Island. *Caution:* You will be paddling past the marina docks and the tour boat docks, so watch for boat traffic.

MILE 1.0: **McDonald Island** has a large dock complex on the southwest end, but this is one of the islands that has a new canoe/kayak campsite (check with the park office in Mallorytown regarding location and signage). There is a beach next to the docks, so you don't have to pay the docking fee, but look out for poison ivy in the brush at the back of the beach.

MILE 1.5: South of McDonald is **Lindsay Island**. Only part of Lindsay is park land; the north side is private property. Round Lindsay on its east side, then go west to **Beaurivage Island**. There are four docking areas and eight campsites on this one small island.

MILE 2.5: **Aubrey** and **Mermaid Islands**, south of Beaurivage, are very pretty islands, with lots of bare granite and wind-bent trees. Aubrey Island is one of the more exposed islands in the group, and if the river is uncomfortably choppy, you may want to skip Aubrey and Mermaid and

Gananoque to the Admiralty Islands

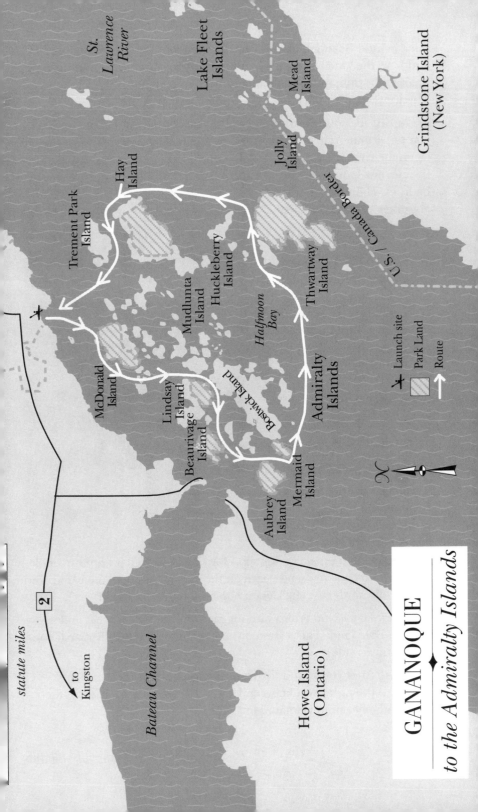

GANANOQUE

to the Admiralty Islands

statute miles

2

to Kingston

Bateau Channel

Howe Island
(Ontario)

*St.
Lawrence
River*

Lake Fleet
Islands

Mead
Island

Jolly
Island

Grindstone Island
(New York)

U.S. / Canada Border

Hay
Island

Trement Park
Island

Mudlunta
Island

Huckleberry
Island

*Halfmoon
Bay*

Thwartway
Island

Admiralty
Islands

McDonald
Island

Lindsay
Island

Beaurivage
Island

Bostwick Island

Aubrey
Island

Mermaid
Island

Launch site

Park Land

Route

duck behind **Bostwick Island** instead. The islands are rocky and steep and have the kind of shoreline that is likely to generate clapotis in rough weather. If you have good weather, turn and paddle eastward to Thwartway (called Leek Island on the topo map of the area).

Sidetrip: At the southeastern end of Bostwick Island (in Halfmoon Bay), you can see the remains of very old potholes. The potholes were created when the river was forced through a narrow channel, and the action of the current spun rocks around and around until they wore holes in the bedrock. Halfmoon Bay is also the location of a "church" where services have been held since 1867. There is an open-air pulpit on a platform by the water where the congregation gathers in boats! There are some classic old photos of residents all decked out in their Sunday best and floating in St. Lawrence River skiffs to hear the service.

MILE 4.5: Thwartway Island has no park facilities except for outhouses and has otherwise been left in a "natural" state. The northern side of the island consists of a short rock wall and doesn't offer good landing spots for kayaks, though it's pretty to look at. There is a rock and sand beach on the southwest side of the island. Turn and paddle north past Huckleberry Island toward **Hay Island**.

MILE 5.5: Hay Island is also without campsites or picnic areas and is partly private land. The section owned by the park is mostly marsh (on the southeast side).

MILE 6.0: After you round the eastern end of Hay Island, turn and paddle to the northwest between Hay and **Tremont Park** Islands, then back to the beach in Gananoque.

Festival of the Islands

In mid-August, Gananoque is host to the Festival of the Islands. It lasts a little over a week and is billed as one of the largest summer celebrations in eastern Ontario. The festival features concerts, amusement rides, skydivers, and a Heritage Days weekend, with historical reenactments and a visit by tall ships. If you're interested in seeing the show—or would just as soon miss it—you should check with the Chamber of Commerce for this year's scheduled dates.

Where to Eat & Where to Stay

RESTAURANTS & LODGING Contact the Gananoque Chamber of Commerce at (800) 561-1595 for a list of restaurants and accommodations. There are a number of high-end B&Bs in Gananoque, but also some inexpensive motels on Highway 2. **CAMPING** There is camping at **Ivy Lea Provincial Park** (east of Gananoque); call (800) 437-2233 for reservations and information. Contact the Gananoque Chamber of Commerce for information about private campgrounds in the area.

Route 33:

━━ ━━ ━━ ━━ ━━ ━━ ━━ ━━ ━━ ━━ ━━ ━━ ━━ ▶

Ivy Lea to the Lake Fleet & Navy Islands

The trip to the Navy Islands is slightly longer than the Admiralty Islands tour, but the reward is a little less hustle and bustle because the islands visited are a little farther out, less inhabited, and farther away from towns.

TRIP HIGHLIGHTS: Good scenery, island hikes, camping.

TRIP RATING:

Beginner: 12-mile trip to the eastern end of the Fleet Islands and back (overnight), or 3-mile day trip to Mulcaster Island and back. *Intermediate:* Add a sidetrip to the Admiralty Islands (Rte. 32) for a total of about 19 miles.

TRIP DURATION: Part day to two days.

NAVIGATION AIDS: NOAA charts 14774 and 14773, Canadian topographic map: *Gananoque* (31C/8) at 1:50,000.

CAUTIONS: Motorboat traffic.

TRIP PLANNING: The longer trip could be done as a brisk day paddle if you like, but it is better as an overnight trip to allow time to explore the island groups. If you are planning on making it an overnighter, see notes on camping in the section introduction. Mulcaster is a popular spot, and if you want to try camping there, grab a site early in the day. Camelot is the only other park island in the Navy or Lake Fleet groups with campsites (it has six), and it is at the end of the route and may require an early start to make it by the end of the day. Another option is Sugar Island, owned by the American Canoe Association, even though it is on the Canadian side. Only ACA members or guests of members can camp here, but there are plenty of campsites available. Reservations are needed only for the "encampment," an annual canoe and kayak get together. For information about Sugar Island, call Jack White at (301) 962–6006. For information about the annual encampment, call the Sugar Island Canoe Club at (201) 986–5815 (Robert Jahn is the contact for the club).

LAUNCH SITE: There is a public ramp in the village of Ivy Lea, but the launch area is very small (no free parking), the ramp steep and narrow, and there is a fee for launching. All in all, you are better off using one of the marinas. Peck's Marina is kayak friendly and is located on Highway 2 (Thousand Islands Parkway), 0.6 mile west of the Ivy Lea exit on Highway 2. There is a daily parking fee to use the lot. Another option is the Misty Isles Lodge, also on the Thousand Islands Parkway, about 6 miles west of the International Bridge. The lodge is less than 2 miles north of Sugar Island and is often used by members of the Sugar Island Canoe Club. It will cost a few dollars a day to leave your car there as well.

Ivy Lea to the Lake Fleet & Navy Islands

DIRECTIONS

START: From **Peck's Marina** just west of Ivy Lea, paddle southwest toward Mulcaster Island.

MILE 1.5: Mulcaster Island is nice but busy. There is of course a picnic shelter, two sets of docks on the east and west sides, a trail that goes around the island, and only three campsites. This is another island that is hard to land on without using the docks. Those doing the day trip to Mulcaster can return to Ivy Lea by the same route, others continue paddling southeast along the chain of islands.

MILE 3.5: Continue southwest around **Downie Island**. The channel between **Stave** and **Prince Regent Islands** is the **Gananoque Narrows**, which is used by many boats, including the tour boats running out of Gananoque. They move back and forth at a pretty good clip, so look both ways before crossing! You are now leaving the **Navy Islands** (named after British officers of the War of 1812) and entering the **Lake Fleet Islands** (named after ships that served in the same war).

MILE 4.5: Stop in at **Sugar Island** for a visit. The main camp is located in the middle the island, but there are campsites all around the island.

MILES 4.5–6.0: The string of small islands between Sugar and Camelot Islands were given a gory set of gunboat names from the War of 1812 (Death, Bloodletter, Axeman, Deathdealer Islands). Don't worry, they are quite harmless and even pleasant to look at.

MILE 6.0: There are no campsites on **Endymion Island**, but the island does have a picnic shelter, dock, and outhouses. **Camelot Island** has six campsites. The docks are on the south side of the island.

MILES 6.0–12.0: Turn around and paddle to the northeast, back to the marina. Take a slightly different path through the many islands for a different view or add one of the sidetrips below for a longer paddle.
Sidetrips: **Thwartway Island:** Paddle west from Camelot to Thwartway Island (see Rte. 32 map). Total distance to and from the island is about 5.0–6.0 miles, more if you go all the way around.
Grindstone Island: The island is just a stone's throw from Camelot, but don't forget the customs rule. If you are starting from the Canadian side it is simpler to just avoid landing, taking your breaks on Camelot or

Ivy Lea to the Lake Fleet & Navy Islands

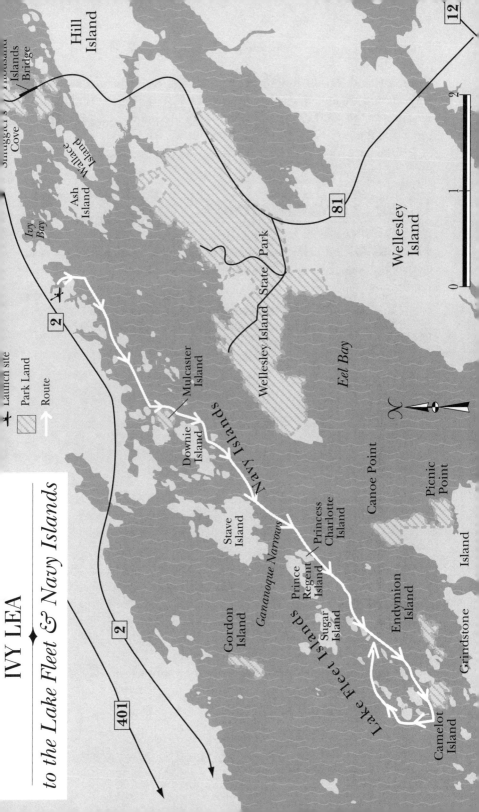

IVY LEA
to the Lake Fleet & Navy Islands

Launch site
Park Land
Route

Thousand Islands Bridge

Smuggler's Cove

Hill Island

Wallace Island

Ash Island

Icy Bay

2

Mulcaster Island

Downie Island

Navy Islands

Wellesley Island State Park

81

Wellesley Island

12

2

Stave Island

Gordon Island

Gananoque Narrows

Prince Regent Island

Princess Charlotte Island

Canoe Point

Eel Bay

Sugar Island

Lake Fleet Islands

Endymion Island

Camelot Island

Grindstone Island

Picnic Point

2

401

0   1   2

Thwartway. At any rate the northwest end of Grindstone has very pretty rock shoreline.

Gordon Island: This is another park island (just 1.0 mile northwest of Sugar Island). Unlike the other islands in the area, Gordon is made of sandstone. The southern tip has a lot of boulders and rocks off shore, but along the rest of the shoreline, you can see the layers of sedimentary rock. There are two docks on the east side and one on the west.

Where to Eat & Where to Stay

RESTAURANTS & LODGING If you are parking at Peck's Marina, there is a restaurant and motel right at the marina. Call (613) 659–3185 for more information. For more information about the **Misty Isles Lodge,** call (613) 382–4232. For a list of restaurants or other accommodations in the area, call the Gananoque Chamber of Commerce at (800) 561–1595. **CAMPING** There is camping at **Ivy Lea Provincial Park** (east of Gananoque). Call (800) 437–2233 for reservations and information. You can also try **Landon Bay Centre,** a private campground, at (613) 382–2719.

Route 34:

━━ ━━ ━━ ━━ ━━ ━━ ━━ ━━ ━━ ━━ ━━ ━━ ━━ ➤

Rockport to Boldt Castle

This trip starts with the scenic village of Rockport on the Canadian side and crosses the St. Lawrence River to visit "Millionaires' Row," an island group with some very, very big cottages. One is the famous Boldt Castle, a turn-of-the-century extravagance that's hard to miss. There are also a lot of pretty island stops and sidetrips along the way.

TRIP HIGHLIGHTS: Good scenery, Boldt Castle.

TRIP RATING:
  Beginner: 6-mile round-trip from Rockport to Heart Island and back.
  Intermediate: 8–16 miles, by adding a trip up to Georgina Island, or south to Grenadier.

TRIP DURATION: Part day to overnight.

NAVIGATION AIDS: NOAA chart 14966, Canadian topographic map 31B/5 at 1:50,000.

CAUTIONS: Boat traffic.

TRIP PLANNING: This route starts in Canada and crosses the border to Boldt Castle. Canadians will have to present a passport when landing on Heart Island, while both Canadians and U.S. citizens will have to deal with going through customs on their return to Rockport. People can avoid this hassle by starting on the U.S. side, but this approach has some problems. The American Channel, which runs along the south bank of the river, is extremely busy with commercial shipping and pleasure boats. It is less of a problem in the spring or fall, but crossing the channel on a busy day could be very bad for your health. A second reason for those from the United States to start at Rockport is that the scenery is better on the Canadian side: more islands and fewer tacky waterfront motels.

LAUNCH SITE: For day trips there is an area in Rockport along the shoulder of the road for parking boats and trailers. There is no charge, but space is limited and no overnight parking is allowed by the ramp. Alternatively you could unload your gear at the ramp and then drop your car off at one of the marinas on the east end of town. If you are going out for an overnight trip in the area, you might consider starting at the Mallorytown Landing, which has a big parking lot for boaters and ramps. There are restrooms next to the parking lot for the tour boat at Rockport.

To get to the public ramp in Rockport, take the Thousand Islands Parkway 2.3 miles east of the International Bridge (Highway 137). Turn south onto the Rockport exit (this road loops through town and then back out to the highway, so you get two chances). Drive 0.2 mile to the boat ramp opposite the tour boat parking lot. There is no charge to launch or park here.

DIRECTIONS

START: From the **Rockport** ramp, paddle slightly east of south, toward the east end of Club Island. *Caution:* Watch out for small boat traffic along the north bank of the river and for tour boats near the Rockport docks.

MILE 0.5: From the tip of Club Island, paddle toward the northeast end of Mary Island.

MILE 1.0: You are now across the border. **Mary Island** is a New York State Park with docks, tent sites, the works. There is a 2-foot gap between Mary Island and the rest of Wellesley Island. Turn and paddle south toward the **Manhattan Island group**.

MILE 2.0: You have a choice of paddling on the south or the north side of the island group. The main shipping channel runs along the U.S. shore here, and if it's busy you may want to paddle the north side and keep the islands between you and all the boat traffic. The area opposite **Alexandria Bay** was known in its heyday as **"Millionaires' Row"** because of extravagant vacation homes and their wealthy owners. Today the area is a little less exclusive, and Millionaires' Row stands opposite another row of tacky econobox motels on the mainland. Paddle southwest along the islands of the Manhattan Group.

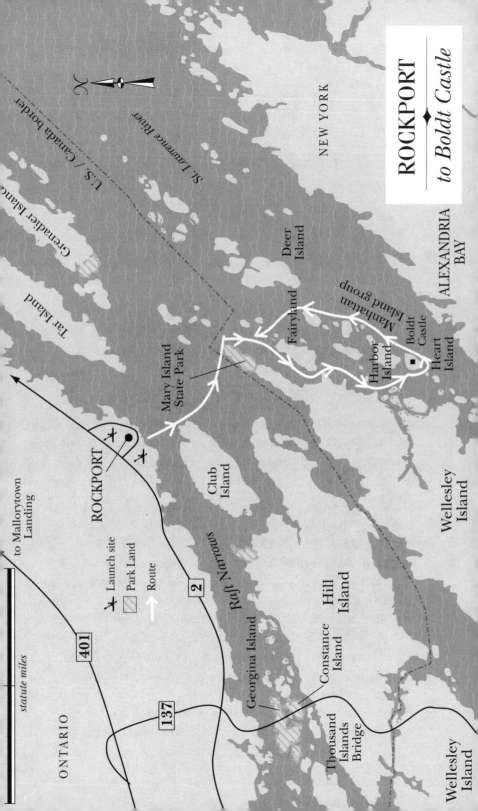

The Castles of the St. Lawrence

For some of the wealthy that built vacation homes in the Thousand Islands, the ideal cottage was a castle. Boldt Castle, open to the public for tours from Victoria Day to Thanksgiving (Canadian Thanksgiving, that is), is the most famous. George Boldt's story is a classic rags to riches tale: He started out as a poor immigrant from Germany and ended up as a millionaire, the owner of the Waldorf Astoria in New York and other hotels around the world. George was apparently quite devoted to his wife, Louise, and began construction of Boldt Castle as a Valentine's Day gift to her. Literally hundreds of workers were employed for several years in constructing the castle, which was to have 120 rooms and eleven buildings in all. The island was renamed and sculpted into the shape of a heart (it was originally called Hart Island). Unfortunately Louise died one year before the castle's scheduled completion in 1904. George ordered the construction stopped and never visited Heart Island again. The unfinished castle was abandoned and sadly decayed until the Thousand Islands Bridge Authority (which also owns the Skydeck Tower) acquired it in 1977 and renovated it as a tourist attraction. For information about Boldt Castle, hours, and admission, call (800) 8–ISLAND.

The other neighborhood castle is Jorstadt Castle on Dark Island (look for tiny Dark Island just off the northeastern end of Grenadier Island). It was designed by the architect Ernest Flagg for Frederick Bourne, the president of the Singer Sewing Machine Company. It was modeled after Scotland's Woodstock Castle and has twenty-eight rooms, five stories, flying buttresses, and reputedly, dungeons. After the original owners died, it was left to the LaSalle Military Academy on Long Island, then sold to the Harold Martin Evangelical Association. It has been used as a private residence and religious retreat since then, and there is a public, nondenominational service every Sunday at 11:00 A.M. It is not otherwise open to the public and is, at the time of writing this, up for sale (currently reduced from $4 million to $2.5 million). Services may no longer be offered if the ownership changes.

MILE 3.0: Boldt Castle is located on **Heart Island**. The customs station is located at the docks on the north side of the island. There is an admission fee to tour the castle. Northwest of Heart Island is the equally huge boathouse for Boldt Castle located on **Wellesley Island** just northwest of Boldt Castle and open to the public. It has several antique wooden boats on display, including some owned by George Boldt.

MILES 3.0–6.0: Follow the same route back to Rockport, or add one of the sidetrips.

Sidetrips: **Georgina Island:** From Club Island, across from Rockport, turn west and paddle down the Raft Narrows. The current will become greater the closer you get to the Thousand Islands Bridge. You will probably want to hug the shore here because the channel can get quite choppy from the boat wakes. The northernmost tip of Hill Island is part of the St. Lawrence Islands National Park; it has a gazebo and picnic area on the waterfront (this is a day-use area only). As you approach the cluster of islands under the bridge, the current will pick up quite a bit. Around the north end of Georgina, the huge eddies and strong current make it hard to go upstream any farther, but Georgina makes a good resting place. There is a little bit of sand beach in the southeast-facing bay, a trail that goes around the island, and a picnic shelter on the east end. There are also a few campsites, although the traffic roaring over the Thousand Islands Bridge is a bit much. Return to Rockport by paddling back down the Raft Narrows. The total distance from Rockport to Georgina and back is about 5.0 miles.

Grenadier Island: From Rockport, or on your way back from Boldt Castle, you can stop at the north end of Grenadier for a break. Although the north end of the island is hard to land on without using the docks, there is a small beach and a campground at Grenadier South. The total distance from Rockport to Grenadier South and back is about 6.0 miles.

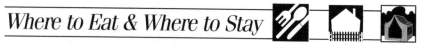

Where to Eat & Where to Stay

RESTAURANTS & LODGING For a list of accommodations on both sides of the river, contact the Thousand Islands International Tourism Council at (800) 8–ISLAND. **CAMPING** For a list of all campgrounds in the area, public and private, call the Tourism Council (or see the phone numbers for the St. Lawrence Islands National Park and New York State Parks given in the section introduction).

Lake Ontario & the St. Lawrence River

New York

Route 35:

▬ ▬ ▬ ▬ ▬ ▬ ▬ ▬ ▬ ▬ ▬ ▬ ▬ ▬ ▬ ➤

Grass Point State Park to Rock Island Light

The navigation aids on the St. Lawrence River are mainly the light-on-a-stick variety, but there are a few exceptions. Besides Rock Island State Park, there are lighthouses at Ogdensburg and Tibbets Point near Cape Vincent. The lighthouse at Rock Island is not open for tours, but the island makes a nice picnic or evening paddle destination. It also has an added attraction for anyone interested in seeing some of the big lake boats go by in the shipping channel just off the island's shore.

TRIP HIGHLIGHTS: Good scenery, lighthouse, and good view of commercial shipping.

TRIP RATING:
  Beginner: 2-mile round-trip from Grass Point to Rock Island and back.

TRIP DURATION: Part day.

NAVIGATION AIDS: USGS: *Thousand Island Park* at 1:24,000, NOAA chart 14773.

CAUTIONS: Motorboat traffic, commercial shipping lanes, rough water due to boat wakes.

TRIP PLANNING: Commercial shipping and personal watercraft can cause problems, but the small island group west of Grass Point can provide shelter from the worst of the mayhem if you paddle on along the south side of the islands. Make sure to stay out of the main channel, which becomes fairly narrow on the south side of Wellesley Island.

LAUNCH SITE: From Highway 81 take the Route 12 exit (just south of the bridge to Wellesley Island). Drive 1.5 miles west on Route 12 to the park entrance on the north side of the road. Follow the road past the beach parking lots and through the campground until you reach the boat ramp next to the marina docks. You will need to buy a day-use permit at the park gate during the peak season. In the early spring or late fall, the park shuts down and fees are not collected though the boat ramp remains open.

DIRECTIONS

START: From the boat ramp at **Grass Point**, paddle northeast toward the islets just off the point. If the river is low, it may be too shallow to paddle between the point and the islands, but as soon as it is deep enough turn to the southwest and paddle toward **Rylstone Island**.

MILE 0.5: These islands are privately owned and have fairly modest cottages, unlike the castles downriver toward Alexandria Bay. Choose a route through the islands, but if there is a lot of boat traffic out in the channel, keep the islands between you and the boats and their wakes.

MILE 1.0: **Rock Island** has a small keepers house, a boathouse and dock, and a lighthouse set on the channel side of the island. There is a small gravel and rock beach next to the lighthouse, though it may be underwater when the river is high. The lighthouse was built in 1882 and belonged to the Coast Guard until 1976 when the island became a state park. The island is fairly open with both bare rock and grass. There are several picnic tables around the island.

MILES 1.0–2.0: Return to Grass Point by the same route.

Where to Eat & Where to Stay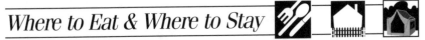

RESTAURANTS & LODGING Plenty of choices in Clayton, just a few miles west of Grass Point State Park. Call the Clayton Chamber of Commerce at (800) 252–9806 for a list, or call (800) 8–ISLAND for listings for the Thousand Islands area in general. **CAMPING** Grass Point State Park has camping available: call (315) 686–4472 for more information about the park, or call (800) 456–CAMP for reservations (recommended if you are visiting during the summer). For information about other state parks along the New York side of the river, call the Thousand Islands State Park Regional Office at (315) 482–2593.

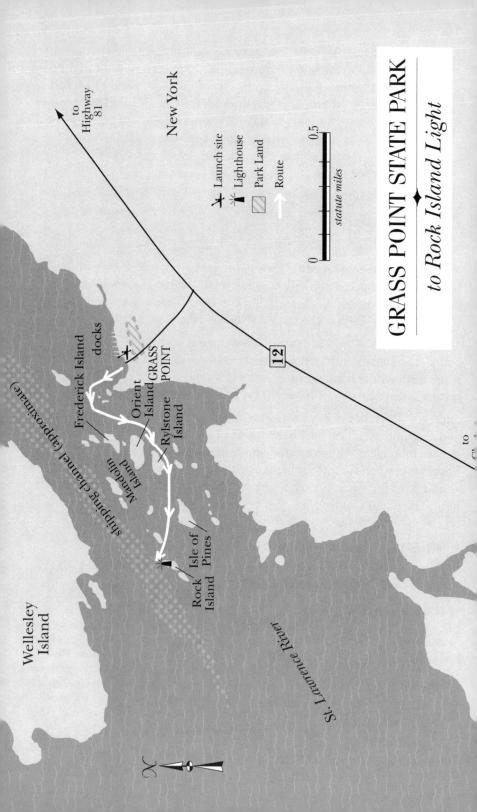

GRASS POINT STATE PARK
◆ to Rock Island Light

✈ Launch site
👁 Lighthouse
▦ Park Land
⬆ Route

statute miles
0   0.5

New York

to Highway 81

Frederick Island

docks

shipping channel (approximate)

Mandolin Island

Orient Island

GRASS POINT

Rylstone Island

Isle of Pines

Rock Island Light

Wellesley Island

St. Lawrence River

12

to

Shipwatching

Watching the Great Lakes ships is a pastime for some people, and it's hard not to be impressed with these monsters when one goes by (at a safe distance, of course). Rock Island is a good place for a nice view without getting too close for comfort. Those interested in finding out more about Great Lakes shipping can try visiting one of the museums devoted to the topic, such as the Army Corps of Engineers Visitor Center and Historical Museum in Duluth and the Marine Museum of the Great Lakes in Kingston. Another great source of information is the Great Lakes and Seaway Shipping Web page, www.oakland.edu/boatnerd/, which has vessel passage lists for various ports and locks around the lakes and photos and names of the ships themselves.

The Antique Boat Museum

Clayton is home to the Antique Boat Museum, which has an excellent collection of old motorboats and other people-powered craft. The St. Lawrence Skiff was developed in this area and widely used by island residents. It was made to be rowed but had no rudder and was instead steered by leaning the boat, a technique with which kayakers and canoeists will be familiar. These are beautiful boats, and many from the turn of the century feature intricate wicker chairs built into them. The museum has an Antique Boat Show the first weekend in August; it has recently added a small craft show, which includes boats and topics of interest to paddlers. For more information about these events or the museum, call (315) 686–4104.

Route 36:

Lakeview State Wildlife Management Area

Lakeview State Wildlife Management Area (SWMA) is located on the eastern shore of Lake Ontario and is typical of the shoreline: low, flat, and sandy, with numerous lagoons along the shore. This type of habitat is a good place to view ducks, and you can make the short portage over the sandbar that separates the inland North Colwell Pond from Lake Ontario. The other side consists of miles and miles of sand beach, and if the wind and waves are right, this is a good place to practice kayak surfing.

TRIP HIGHLIGHTS: Good waterfowl habitat and viewing, surfing.

TRIP RATING:
   Beginner: 2-mile paddle around the lake, plus optional portage over to the lakeside.
   Intermediate: Same tour, with surfing on the lakeshore if conditions are favorable.

TRIP DURATION: Part day.

NAVIGATION AIDS: USGS: *Ellisburg* at 1:24,000.

CAUTIONS: Potential for rip currents along shore in strong wind.

TRIP PLANNING: Probably the only time to avoid this trip is during duck hunting season. Otherwise the inner pond is very protected, even in bad weather. As with all lakeside marshes, be aware that water levels change seasonally and with the occasional seiche, so that marshes may be different from what is shown on maps.

LAUNCH SITE: From Interstate 81 exit at Sandy Creek and go west on County 15 to Sandy Pond Corners. Take Route 3 north for 5.8

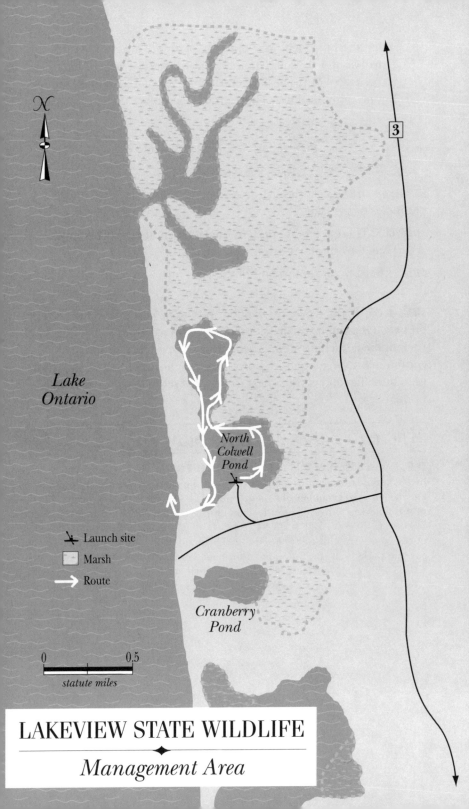

N

Lake
Ontario

*North
Colwell
Pond*

Launch site
Marsh
Route

*Cranberry
Pond*

0   0.5
statute miles

LAKEVIEW STATE WILDLIFE
Management Area

3

miles, then turn left/west onto the road with a brown SWMA sign. Drive west for 0.7 mile, then turn north at the entrance to Lakeview SWMA. There is a boat launching area and parking lot, but no other facilities. There are no fees to park here or launch.

DIRECTIONS

START: From the **Lakeview** launching area, paddle north around the perimeter of the lake.

MILE 0.5: There is a bottleneck in the lake here that may be impassable at low water. Continue north if you can.

MILE 1.0: At the northern end of the lake, turn and paddle south along the shore.

MILE 1.75: Portage over the sandbar (100–200 yard carry) and launch on **Lake Ontario**. If you are skipping the portage, turn and paddle east back to the launching area. *Sidetrip:* You can extend your paddle by continuing north along the shore—0.2 mile north of the portage there is an inlet that allows you access to the next set of marshes without a portage.

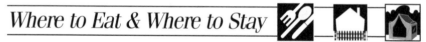

Where to Eat & Where to Stay

RESTAURANTS & LODGING For information on nearby accommodations and restaurants, contact the chambers for the following areas: Greater Oswego Chamber of Commerce: (315) 343–7681, Cape Vincent Chamber of Commerce: (315) 654–2481, Henderson Harbor: (315) 628–5046, Sackets Harbor: (315) 646–1700 **CAMPING** There are several state parks in the area. For reservations call (800) 456–2267 (for all parks), or for information about specific parks, call the following: **Burnham Point:** (315) 654–2324, **Long Point:** (315) 649–5258, **Westcott Beach:** (315) 646–2239, **Southwick Beach:** (315) 846–5338. Reservations are recommended between Memorial Day and Labor Day.

Route 37:

━━ ━━ ━━ ━━ ━━ ━━ ━━ ━━ ━━ ━━ ━━ ━━ ━━ ━━ ⟶

Chimney Bluffs State Park

This trip is a short paddle along a strange landscape—it almost looks like the Badlands with water. Although most of the south shore of Lake Ontario is pretty flat, the eroded spires and cliffs of Chimney Bluffs make for an interesting change.

TRIP HIGHLIGHTS: Good scenery.

TRIP RATING:

> *Beginner:* 2-mile trip along Chimney Bluffs and back.

TRIP DURATION: Part day.

NAVIGATION AIDS: USGS: *Sodus Point* at 1:24,000

CAUTIONS: Shoreline exposed to wind and waves.

TRIP PLANNING: The critical factor for this trip is choosing a good day. The shoreline offers no good sheltered landing spots, and in some places the steep bluffs come almost down to the water; in many sections the beaches are steep and have large boulders just off shore. Wait for a calm day and check the marine forecast before setting out.

LAUNCH SITE: From the intersection of Highways 104 and 414, take Lake Bluff Road north (Lake Bluff Road continues north from where 414 ends at 104). Drive north for 3.6 miles, then continue straight through the intersection with the stop sign (Lake Bluff Road changes to Garner Road here). Follow Garner Road for another 2.7 miles as it turns east and intersects with East Bay Road. Turn north (left) onto East Bay Road and drive 1.0 mile to the parking lot and turnaround at the lakeshore. There is no fee to park or launch here; there are also no toilets or other facilities. It is a short carry down to the water.

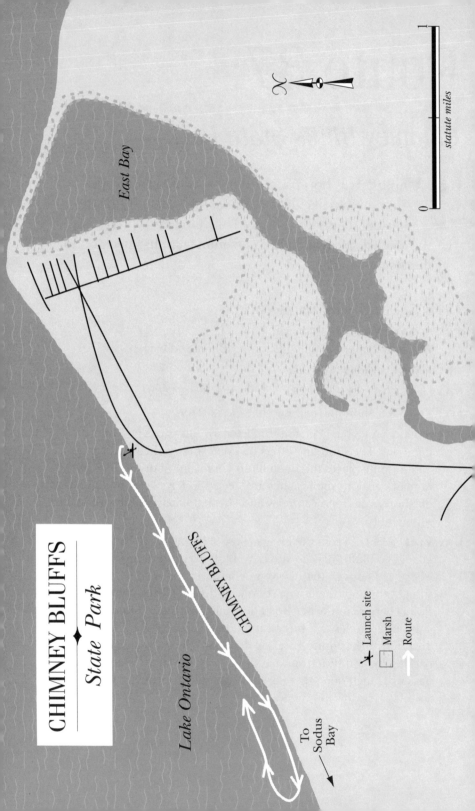

CHIMNEY BLUFFS
State Park

East Bay

statute miles

0

Lake Ontario

CHIMNEY BLUFFS

To
Sodus
Bay

✈ Launch site
☐ Marsh
⬆ Route

Drumlin Country

Chimney Bluffs are actually the remains of drumlins that are being eroded gradually by waves and weather. Drumlins are glacial formations created when the movement of an ice sheet over the earth pushes loose gravel, sand, and stones into distinctive hills. Drumlins are typically about 100 feet high, blunt and wide at one end, and long and tapered at the other; the ice moved from the blunt to the tapered end. Drumlins are found in groups called drumlin fields, and the west-central portion of New York State contains the largest drumlin field in the United States.

DIRECTIONS

START: Paddle west from the **Chimney Bluffs** launch site. The strange looking chimney formations continue along the shore for about 1.0 mile. There is a hiking trail along the top of the ridge, and you may see some people up there.

MILE 1.0: After the bluff ends, the shoreline becomes low and brushy. Paddle back to the launch site the way that you came. *Sidetrips:* For a longer paddle, continue west from the end of the bluffs for another 1.5 mile, then turn south into **Sodus Bay**, a large and protected bay. There are a number of marinas and many private homes along the shore. Or from the launch site, paddle east along the shoreline. A very short portage will get you over the gravel bar that separates East Bay from Lake Ontario.

Where to Eat & Where to Stay

RESTAURANTS & LODGING For a list of lodging and restaurants in the area, call the Finger Lakes Travel Association at (800) 866–5900. **CAMPING** Chimney Bluffs State Park does not have a campground, but **Fairhaven State Park** does. Call (315) 947–5205 for more information about the park or (800) 456–CAMP for reservations.

Route 38:

▬ ▬ ▬ ▬ ▬ ▬ ▬ ▬ ▬ ▬ ▬ ▬ ▬ ▬ ▬ ▬ ➤

Rochester: Irondequoit Bay

Irondequoit Bay in Rochester is typical of many bays along the south shore of Lake Ontario and has a sand/gravel bar across the lakeside end and wetlands/marshes at the south end. It makes an interesting paddle by itself, and the cut through the barrier that leads out into the lake provides good access to the lakeshore as well. Once heavily industrialized, Irondequoit Bay is now a pleasant mix of park and residential land. The bluffs along the east side of the bay make for a scenic urban paddle, and, if conditions are right, the lakeshore outside of the bay makes a good place to try surfing.

TRIP HIGHLIGHTS: Good scenery, marshes, surfing.

TRIP RATING:
Beginner: 8-mile paddle from Irondequoit Creek to Seabreeze Park and back.
Intermediate: Practice surfing along the beach east of the entrance to Irondequoit Bay.

TRIP DURATION: Part to full day

NAVIGATION AIDS: NOAA chart 14815, USGS: *Rochester East* at 1:24,000.

CAUTIONS: Boat traffic, clapotis at entrance to Irondequoit Bay.

TRIP PLANNING: There are marinas on Irondequoit Bay, and you can certainly expect a lot of boat traffic on summer weekends. For a quieter paddle, try weekday, evening, or off-season paddling.

LAUNCH SITE: The city has recently purchased land near Irondequoit Creek and has plans for a public boat launch there. Until then, paddlers can put in at the Bay Creek Paddling Center, which has a dock and launch area right on the creek. Parking for the day costs a few dollars. To get there, take Empire Boulevard/Highway 104 to Irondequoit Bay, just northeast of central Rochester. The launch area is just east of the bridge over Irondequoit Creek (at 1099 Empire Boulevard). There is a parking lot next to the building and a rest room in the store.

DIRECTIONS

START: Paddle east from the mouth of **Irondequoit Creek** out into the bay. If the water is low, paddle between the white pole channel markers where the water is deepest.

MILES 0.0–1.0: You will probably want to paddle up one side or the other of **Irondequoit Bay** to avoid the motorboat traffic at the busier times. The land on either side is part of **Irondequoit Bay Park** (East and West).

MILE 2.0: If you want you can paddle into **Held's Cove** and check out the islands there. There are a few cottages on the islands and shore. The

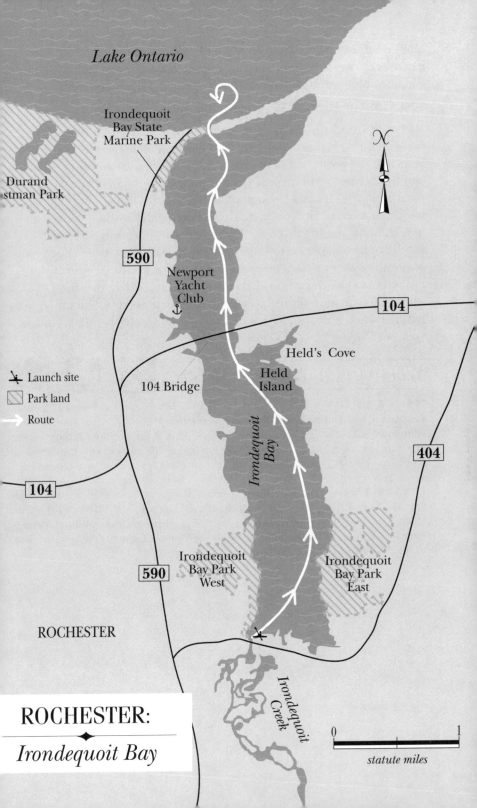

Lake Ontario

Irondequoit
Bay State
Marine Park

Durand
stman Park

590

Newport
Yacht
Club

104

104 Bridge

Held's Cove

Held
Island

⚓ Launch site

▨ Park land

→ Route

Irondequoit Bay

104

404

Irondequoit
Bay Park
West

590

Irondequoit
Bay Park
East

ROCHESTER

Irondequoit Creek

ROCHESTER:
Irondequoit Bay

0   1

statute miles

bluffs on the east side of the river are highest along this stretch of the east shore. They are composed of compacted sand and gravel as are the Chimney Bluffs, and are also being eroded along the waterfront.

MILE 2.5: The **Highway 104 bridge** crosses the river here.

MILE 4.0: Irondequoit Bay State Marine Park is a narrow little park between the west shore of the bay and Highway 590. There is a state boat launch at the north end of the park. At this point you can turn around and head back to Irondequoit Creek by the same route, or you can paddle out the channel leading to the lakeshore. *Caution:* The channel is narrow and has vertical walls, making it pretty choppy when there is a lot of boat traffic passing through. Also, if you are going outside to surf, watch out for the clapotis along the breakwall. It will be better once you get past the area where waves are reflected off the walls. *Sidetrip:* If you just want to extend your paddle, try paddling west along the shore. About 1.0 mile west of the entrance to Irondequoit Bay is Durand Eastman Park, and another 3.0 miles will bring you to the mouth of the Genesee River.

Where to Eat & Where to Stay

RESTAURANTS & LODGING The **Newport House Restaurant and Marina** is on the west side of Irondequoit Bay just south of the Highway 104 Bridge. They serve a lot of seafood, but this is probably not a good place to walk in wearing your wet suit. For more information call the Newport House at (716) 467–8480. For accommodations and restaurants in the Rochester area, call the Greater Rochester Visitors Association at (800) 677–7282.
CAMPING **Hamlin Beach** is located west of Rochester on the Lake Ontario State Parkway. For information about the park, call (716) 964–2462 or (800) 456–CAMP for reservations. There is also camping at the **Webster County Park** located east of Irondequoit Bay. Call the Webster Chamber of Commerce at (716) 265–3960 for more information.

Lake Ontario & the St. Lawrence River

Québec

Saguenay–St. Lawrence Marine Park & Parc du Saguenay (Les Parcs Québécois)

A t Tadoussac, Quebec, two huge rivers collide: the St. Lawrence and the Saguenay. Both of these great rivers are saltwater estuaries and are greatly influenced by tides. The colliding river and tide currents create rich upwellings of krill, which has made this one of the richest feeding areas on the planet for marine mammals. This rich food supply and the deep water near shore allow visitors to see minke whales, finback whales, St. Lawrence beluga whales, and the occasional blue whale while paddling along the coast. The Saguenay–St. Lawrence Marine Park contains well over 400 square miles of protected coastal waters along the St. Lawrence from Les Escoumins to just south of Port-au-Saumon.

The Parc du Saguenay includes nearly all of the Saguenay River shoreline from Saint-Fulgence to Tadoussac. The Saguenay Fjord is an ancient river valley, carved into steep cliffs by glacial ice. The spectacular beauty of the fjord reaches inland for nearly 60 miles from the rivers' confluence with the St. Lawrence. Kayakers can not only enjoy the scenery of the fjord, but with luck they will get to see the endangered St. Lawrence beluga whales that come up the fjord to feed.

Taudoussac is located in the heart of French Canada, about 120 miles northeast of Québec City. Do not make the mistake of thinking that you are in a bilingual country anymore—even at tourist information centers you rarely find someone available who speaks fluent English. Even those who speak French fluently may have some problems sorting through the Québécois accent. Bring a phrase book or, ideally, a friend who speaks French. Don't worry, though; hospitality is a way of life here, and people are very patient in helping you learn their language. Enjoying the unique French-Canadian culture of the region is one of the most delightful parts of the visit, so if you are an Anglophone, don't let this keep you away.

Route 39:

▬ ▬ ▬ ▬ ▬ ▬ ▬ ▬ ▬ ▬ ▬ ▬ ▬ ➡

Baie Sainte-Marguerite to Anse-de-Roche

Paddling in the fjord is a great trip for paddlers of all skill levels. The relatively warm water of the river and the narrow width of the fjord (1–2 miles) produces a relatively sheltered body of water in a beautiful fjord with high ridges and cliffs that reach heights of almost 1,000 feet. At Baie Sainte-Marguerite a river empties into the fjord and creates a rich feeding area for beluga whales that come up the fjord from the St. Lawrence. Although commonly sighted in the area, the St. Lawrence beluga whales are an endangered species and only about 300 whales remain in the entire waterway. For this reason it is illegal to seek out beluga whales or to approach them by boat. However they are curious animals, and if you paddle in the area, it is likely that a group of whales will come to have a closer look at your kayak. In summer 1998, a group of kayakers with Caribou Expeditions was treated to a family of beluga whales swimming under their kayaks and hovering right under their boats, eyeing them from just a few feet away.

TRIP HIGHLIGHTS: Beautiful fjord scenery, beluga whales, lovely undeveloped shoreline.

TRIP RATING:

    Beginner/Intermediate: 8–9 miles one way, Baie Sainte-Marguerite to Anse des Îslets-Rouges to Anse-de-Roche.

TRIP DURATION: Day or part day. Overnight camping is an option.

NAVIGATION AIDS: Les Parcs Québécois Park du Saguenay brochure map, Canadian topographic map 22 C/4.

CAUTIONS: Cliff walls may funnel high winds from the east or west.

TRIP PLANNING: If you plan to camp overnight, check with the visitor center in La Baie regarding permits or reservations.

TIDE INFORMATION: You can get a rough indication of expected tides and tide currents from tide tables for Tadoussac. The tide current in this area of the Saguenay Fjord is usually about 1 knot or less, and you can work up back eddies along the shore or move to midchannel to catch the full flow, depending on your desired direction of travel. Mean tides at Tadoussac are about 12 feet, so shoreline appearance may vary greatly, depending on whether you arrive at high tide or low tide.

LAUNCH SITES:

Anse-de-Roche: From Tadoussac head north on Highway 138, then turn west on Highway 172 and follow the road for 9.2 miles. Watch for the sign for L'Anse-de-Roche and follow this road south to the Saguenay. As soon as you see the water, turn right on the small paved road and follow it to the small marina and dock. A boat ramp and parking are available. There are bathrooms and a restaurant at the marina.

Baie Sainte-Marguerite: From Tadoussac head north on Highway 138, then turn west on Highway 172 and follow the road for 14 miles. After crossing the river twice, turn left at the Parc du

Baie Sainte-Marguerite to Anse-de-Roche

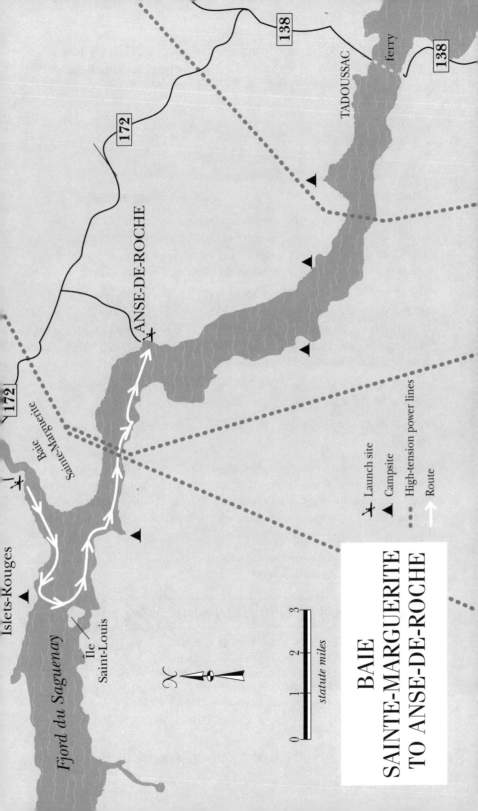

TADOUSSAC

ferry

138

138

172

ANSE-DE-ROCHE

172

Baie Sainte-Marguerite

172

Islets-Rouges

Île Saint-Louis

Fjord du Saguenay

✈ Launch site

▲ Campsite

High-tension power lines

⬆ Route

N

statute miles

0   1   2   3

BAIE
SAINTE-MARGUERITE
TO ANSE-DE-ROCHE

Saguenay/Baie Sainte-Marguerite access road. You can drive to within 300 feet of the water. Park in the large parking lot after unloading boats. There are outhouse rest room facilities but no potable water.

DIRECTIONS

START: From Baie Sainte-Marguerite head west along the shore.

MILE 1.5: As you near the mouth of the bay, watch for beluga whales. Where the water from the Rivière Sainte-Marguerite mixes with the Saguenay, a rich brackish water feeding area is produced. Again, NEVER pursue or approach these endangered whales. Let them come to you if they are in the mood to visit your group.

MILE 2.0: Continuing west you come to rock shelf and sand and gravel beach (depending on tide level) where there is a campsite with a tent platform. This is a nice place to take a break or have lunch. This small cove is called **Anse-des-Îslets-Rouges**.

MILE 3.5: From Anse-des-Îslets-Rouges, head south across the fjord passing by **Île-Saint-Louis** to the south shore of the fjord.

MILE 5.0: At Mile 5.0 there is a small bay with another **water access campsite**.

MILE 7.0: Heading east along the south shore of the fjord, you pass along a beautiful rocky coast. Passing along a cliff wall, you paddle under huge high-tension wires that cross over the entire span of the fjord. At about Mile 7.0 there is a nice flat rock shelf and/or a sand and gravel beach (depending on the tide), which is a good spot to take a break.

MILE 9.0: Continue east down the fjord and then cross to its other side to the marina at **Anse-de-Roche**.

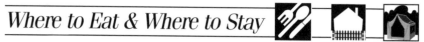

Where to Eat & Where to Stay

RESTAURANTS & LODGING   This is a resort area; there are several restaurant and lodging choices in Tadoussac. For information call the Saguenay–Lac-Saint-Jean Tourist Association at (800) 463–9651. **CAMPING** Within the **Parc du Saguenay** are many options for developed campsites and rustic water access only campsites. For information call the park at (418) 544–7388.

Route 40:

━ ━ ━ ━ ━ ━ ━ ━ ━ ━ ━ ━ ━ ━ ━ ━ ➤

Tadoussac to Grandes Bergeronnes

From Tadoussac to Grandes Bergeronnes is a beautiful stretch of coast with both rocky shores and large coastal sand dune bluffs. It is also an excellent area to see whales. By staying relatively near shore, the trip requires only intermediate skills; however, just a short distance offshore, the tide currents running out of the Saguenay fjord can be as high as 7.0 knots, and where these powerful currents meet with the St. Lawrence, they form rapids miles offshore. The turbulent waters where the giant rivers collide

provide an abundance of food for marine mammals, but unless you have advanced paddling skills, it is best to watch it from a safe distance. With the abundance of food and deep water just beyond the tide banks, you will almost certainly see minke or beluga whales on your trip. With luck you may get close to a huge fin whale or even the rare blue whale. Do not make sudden changes to your course to approach them. Let them come to you. To learn more about the whales and seals in the area, make sure you visit the Marine Mammal Museum in Tadoussac before you start your trip. You can get a copy of the whale-watching rules from the Marine Mammal Protection Act at the museum.

TRIP HIGHLIGHTS: Beautiful rocky coast, huge dune bluffs, seals, and minke, beluga, and fin whales.

TRIP RATING:
Intermediate: 10-mile trip one way from Tadoussac to Grandes Bergerones.

TRIP DURATION: Day or part day.

NAVIGATION AIDS: CHS chart LC1235, Canadian topographical map 22 C/4.

CAUTIONS: Extremely cold water, strong tide currents near the mouth of the Saguenay, tide overfalls and rapids 1–3 miles offshore, steep waves or breaking waves when seas run counter to current.

TRIP PLANNING: Start your trip close to high tide. If you try to paddle out of the Saguenay when tide currents are running up river, you will not be able to make progress even near shore. At the maximum outflow, the tide current in the center of the Saguenay runs up to 7 knots. The outflow of the St. Lawrence peaks at up to 4 knots at a distance of 3–4 miles from shore. Currents near shore are much more moderate. Winds from the northeast or southwest have a very long fetch and can generate very steep difficult seas, especially when waves run against the tide currents. Kayakers who paddle too far out into the Saguenay could be pushed miles offshore and be swept through rapids and tidal overfalls. A chart is a requirement to understand the tidal currents and the direction of water flow that can spin 360 degrees over a full tide cycle in some areas. Also note the tide flats near Grandes Bergeronnes, which extend about 0.5 mile from shore. Don't get caught on the flats at low tide, but note you can enter the harbor along the buoyed channel to Grandes Bergeronnes at low tide. A wet suit or dry suit is strongly recommended because summer water temperatures range from the high 30s to low 40s °F.

TIDE INFORMATION: CHS chart LC1235 has current speed and direction information for the St. Lawrence. Mean tides at Tadoussac are 12 feet.

LAUNCH SITES:

Tadoussac: In Tadoussac launch from the beach in the harbor. There is a road and a concrete boat ramp that goes through the seawall in the harbor. After unloading the boats on the beach, park back in town. Parking can be a problem—so plan to park in one of the paid lots for about $3.00. There are public bathrooms up the hill (toward the large hotel with the red tin roof).

Grandes Bergeronnes: From Tadoussac head north on Highway 138 for about 12 miles to the town of Grandes Bergeronnes. From 138 follow the signs to the Centre Archeo Topo (Museum of Archeology), which is located at the marina, about 1 mile from the highway. Bathrooms, changing rooms, and showers are available at the marina. There is a $2.00 kayak-launching fee. Submit the fee and a float plan to the harbormaster. In summer this is a very busy spot and parking can be limited. You may want to run your shuttle early in the day to ensure that parking is not a problem.

DIRECTIONS

START: From the **beach** in Tadoussac Harbour, head east out into the **St. Lawrence.** You need to start when water is flowing out of the Saguenay because the in-flowing tide current may be too swift to allow you to paddle into the river. *Caution:* At maximum flow tide currents mid-channel on the Saguenay can run as high as 7 knots. Stay near shore to minimize the current and avoid being pushed miles offshore.

MILE 1.0: After about 1.0 mile you round the rocky headland of **Pointe Rouge.** If you are wrong about the tides and water is flowing into the Saguenay, you may not be able to pass this point. Continue east along the coast.

MILE 2.0: Beyond Pointe Rouge the shore transitions from rocky coast to sand dune bluffs. At **Pointe aux Vaches** there are high, steep dune bluffs at the water's edge. After rounding the point, you follow the coast, now heading northeast.

GRAND
BERGERONNES

Pointe à John
marina public access

Pointe Sauvac

138

*Baie des
Petites Bergeronnes*

*Rivière des
Petite Bergeronnes*

St. Lawrence River

Pointe
à la
Carriole

*Cap de
Granite*

Launch site

Tide Flats (dry at low tide)

Route

La Grande
Anse

overfall rapids
with outflow

*Baie du
Moulin à Baude*

*Rivière
Moulin à Baude*

Pointe
aux Vaches

138

Pointe
Rouge

*Baie
Sainte-Cath*

0   1

one statute mile

172

TADOUSSAC

ferry

Pointe
Noire

Rivière Saguenay

TADOUSSAC TO
GRANDES BERGERONNES

MILE 3.0: At **Baie du Moulin à Baude**, there is a nice sand beach to stop and take a break. Here the steep dune bluffs are hundreds of feet high. Enjoy your stop, but don't stay too long, or you may get caught on the tide flat at low tide.

MILE 3.25: Leaving the bay you pass a small river, **Rivière Moulin à Baude**, with lovely cascading falls at the edge of the water.

MILE 4.0: Just past the cascade you round a point and enter a cove with high rock cliffs. This beautiful cove is called **La Grande Anse**.

MILES 5.0–9.0: Beyond the granite shores of La Grande Anse is a lower shoreline with some sand and gravel beaches that are available to land at midtide levels. *Caution:* The tide banks extend about 1,000 to 1,500 feet from the shore at high tide, so you may hit boulders far from land in the shallow water.

MILE 9.0: You reach **Baie des Petites Bergeronnes**. Do not enter the bay on a falling tide because you are likely to get stranded on the tide flats. Keeping 0.5 mile offshore, continue around **Pointe Sauvac** to **Grandes Bergeronnes**.

MILE 10.0: If you are at or near low tide, make sure you follow the buoyed channel into the marina and boat ramp at Grandes Bergeronnes. *Caution:* Watch out for small craft traffic. There will probably be many high-speed Zodiac whale-watching boats entering or leaving the channel.

Where to Eat & Where to Stay

RESTAURANTS   There is a small cafe at the marina in Grandes Bergeronnes, and there are three restaurants 1 mile away in the small town of Grandes Bergeronnes. For information call the Corporation Touristique de Bergeronnes at (418) 232–6326. There are also several restaurants in Tadoussac: For more information call the Saguenay–Lac-Saint-Jean Tourist Association at (800) 463–9651. **LODGING**   There are many options for lodging in the Tadoussac area. For information call the Saguenay–Lac-Saint-Jean Tourist Association at (800) 463–9651. **CAMPING**   Within the **Parc du Saguenay** there are many options for developed campsites and water access only rustic campsites. For information call the park at (418) 544–7388. For camping closer to Tadoussac or Bergeronnes, you will need to rely on private campgrounds. There are many in the region. One of the best is at **Bon-Désir**, with large campsites and a great view of the coast near Cap de Bon-Désir. Not only can you watch the whales from your campsite, but there is water access for kayakers. (The bank is a bit steep and slippery, and you must launch at high to midtide, but it is still an acceptable put-in point.) Call (418) 232–6297 for information.

Tadoussac to Grandes Bergeronnes

Route 41:

━━ ━━ ━━ ━━ ━━ ━━ ━━ ━━ ━━ ━━ ━━ ➤

Grandes Bergeronnes to Les Escoumins

From Grandes Bergeronnes to les Escoumins is a beautiful stretch of coast with rocky shores, a historic lighthouse, and great whale watching. The route takes you around Cap de Bon-Désir, a lovely granite headland that has been set up by the marine park as a whale observation point for visitors. To learn more about the whales and seals in the area, make sure you visit the Marine Mammal Museum in Tadoussac before you start your trip, and stop in at Cap de Bon-Désir to see the lighthouse and the small museum as well. Boats are required by law to stay 1 kilometer off of the point to prevent them from disturbing the whales that come close to shore (where park visitors observe them). The rule is rarely if ever enforced for sea kayakers. However, in fairness to the visitors on shore, you should swing wide as you round the point. Boat-watchers can watch huge ships pause to pick up St. Lawrence pilots from the pilot station near Escoumins to help them pilot the river between here and Montreal. For this reason international shipping comes quite close to shore.

TRIP HIGHLIGHTS: Beautiful rocky coast, international shipping traffic, seals, and minke, beluga, and fin whales.

TRIP RATING:
  Intermediate: 12 miles one way from Grandes Bergeronnes to Les Escoumins.

TRIP DURATION: Day or part day.

NAVIGATION AIDS: CHS chart LC1235, Canadian topographical maps 22 C/4 and 22 C/6.

CAUTIONS: Extremely cold water, shallow boulders at the edge of the tide banks, tide currents up to 2 knots, steep waves or breaking waves when seas run counter to current.

TRIP PLANNING: You can launch from Grandes Bergeronnes at high or low tide. Tide currents 1 or 2 miles from shore in this part of the St. Lawrence are 1–2 knots, but much less near shore. Review the tide current information from your chart if you want to make use of the tide currents, but you can complete your trip without undue effort even running against the flow if you stay near shore. Winds from the northeast or southwest have a very long fetch and can generate very steep, difficult seas, especially when waves run against the tide currents. A chart is a requirement to understand the tidal currents; the direction of water flow can spin 360 degrees over a full tide cycle in some areas. Also note the tide flats near Grandes Bergeronnes that extend about 0.5 mile from shore. Don't get caught on the flats at low tide; you can, however, enter or leave the harbor along the buoyed channel at Grandes Bergeronnes at low tide. A wet suit or dry suit is strongly recommended because summer water temperatures range from the high 30s to low 40s °F.

TIDE INFORMATION: CHS chart LC1235 has current speed and direction information for the St. Lawrence. Mean tides at Tadoussac are approximately 12 feet.

LAUNCH SITES:

Grandes Bergeronnes: See Route 40: Tadoussac to Grandes Bergeronnes.

Les Escoumins: From Highway 138 you pass through Escoumins. With the bay on your right, take the next right on Rue Saint Marcellin, then right again on Rue de la Croix to the municipal park at Pointe-de-la-Croix. There is a boat ramp and parking, but no bathroom facilities or potable water available here. The park is easy to see from a distance as there is a large metal cross lit at night with electric lights.

DIRECTIONS

START: From **Grandes Bergeronnes** head out the channel past the edge of the tide banks and turn northeast to follow the coast to Escoumins. *Caution:* Watch out for small craft traffic because whale-watching tour operaters use the harbor, and many high-speed Zodiacs enter or leave the harbor in summer.

MILE 2.0: Paddling near the edge of the tide banks near Grandes Bergeronnes is an excellent way to see beluga and minke whales. About 2.0 miles down the coast, there is a sand and gravel beach, which at midtide is a good kayak landing. Use caution because there may be shallow water or boulders far from shore near the edge of the tide banks.

MILE 5.5: Between the beach and Cap de Bon-Désir is a wide boulder-strewn tide flat that is up to 0.75 mile wide. Don't get caught on the flat at low tide—it is a long, slippery hike over boulders, seaweed, and rounded cobbles to get to shore or deep water. You pass by Bon-Désir private campground as you head to Cap de Bon-Désir. At Mile 5.5 you reach **Cap de Bon-Désir**, a lovely granite headland with a lighthouse and a whale observation area. By law boats are supposed to stay one kilometer (0.62 mile) offshore to allow whales to pass close to shore undisturbed. Although this rule is rarely enforced for kayakers, you should swing wide of shore for the sake of the land-bound visitors. The point and the deep water near shore make this an excellent spot to view minke, beluga, or fin whales.

MILE 6.5: About 1.0 mile past Cap de Bon-Désir, you come to **Anse à la Cave**, a cove with a sand and gravel beach suitable for landing kayaks at most tide levels. This is a good place to stop because the next few miles are granite rock with very few places to land.

MILE 9.5: Continuing northeast past Anse à la Cave, the shore consists of solid granite, so plan to stay in your boat for the next 2.0 miles. Watch for a huge radar tower. This is the Centre de Trafic Maritime, which coordinates shipping on this part of the St. Lawrence. At Mile 9.5 there

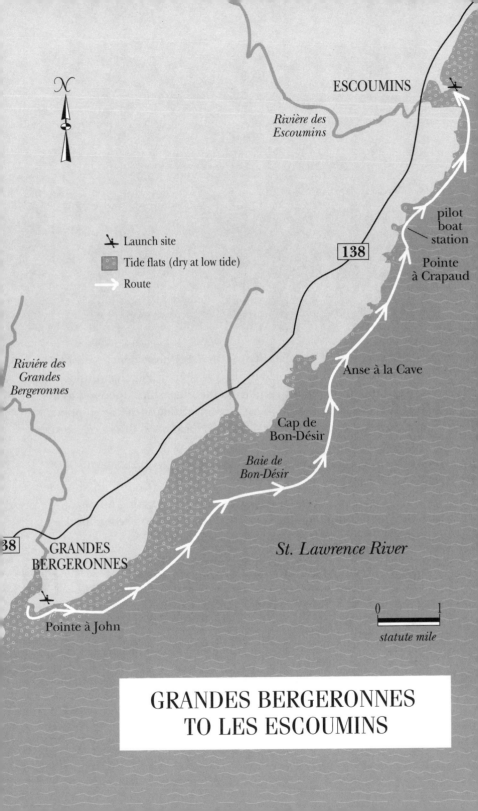

N

⚓ Launch site
▨ Tide flats (dry at low tide)
→ Route

ESCOUMINS

Rivière des Escoumins

138

pilot boat station

Pointe à Crapaud

Rivière des Grandes Bergeronnes

Anse à la Cave

Cap de Bon-Désir

Baie de Bon-Désir

38

GRANDES BERGERONNES

St. Lawrence River

Pointe à John

0   1
statute mile

GRANDES BERGERONNES TO LES ESCOUMINS

is a nice cove with a sand beach; you can land easily here at most tide levels. Here is the harbor used by the Laurentian Pilotage Authority for the boats that ferry pilots to and from the huge ships upbound to the Great Lakes or downbound to the Atlantic. Because all the shipping must pause here to pick up or drop off a local pilot, this is a great spot for boat-watchers.

MILE 11.5: Just beyond the pilot station is a large rocky cove with a nice sand beach. Past the beach is the Escoumins Dive Centre, so don't be surprised if you see scuba divers as well as seals popping up next to your kayak. The beautiful granite rock coast continues to **Escoumins**. Head for the large metal cross next to the boat ramp.

Where to Eat & Where to Stay

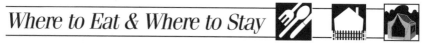

RESTAURANTS   There is a small cafe at the marina in Grandes Bergeronnes, and there are three restaurants a mile away in the small town of Grandes Bergeronnes. Escoumins also has a few restaurants, with the **Petite Royale** being a good choice for seafood at reasonable prices. For information call the Corporation Touristique de Bergeronnes at (418) 232–6326 and the Saguenay–Lac-Saint-Jean Tourist Association at (800) 463–9651. **LODGING** There are many options for lodging in the Tadoussac area. For information call the Saguenay–Lac-Saint-Jean Tourist Association at (800) 463–9651. **CAMPING** See Route 40: Tadoussac to Grandes Bergeronnes.

Appendix A: Kayak Clubs in the Great Lakes Region & Canada

American Canoe Association
www.aca-paddler.org/

Canadian Recreational Canoe Association
www.crca.ca/

Cataraqui Canoe Club
P.O. Box 1882
Kingston, ON K7L 5J7
Club telephone (recorded info): +1
(613) 544–8375
www.fox.nstn.ca/~nicholls/ccc.html

Chicago Area Sea Kayakers
4019 North Narrangansett
Chicago, IL 60634
www.prairienet.org/paddling/clubs/
caska.html

**Finger Lakes-Ontario Watershed
Paddlers' Club (FLOW)**
264 Vollmer Parkway
Rochester, NY 14623

Great Lakes Sea Kayaking Club
3712 Shallow Brook
Bloomfield Hills, MI 48013
www.threecat.netgate.net/glskc/
glskc1.htm

Great Lakes Sea Kayaking Association
(GLSKA)
P.O. Box 22082
45 Overlea Boulevard
Toronto, ONT M4H 1N9 Canada
www.geocities.com/Yosemite/Gorge/
4657/

International Klepper Society
P.O. Box 973
Good Hart, MI 49737

Lansing Oar and Paddle Club
P.O. Box 26254
Lansing, MI 48909

Mad City Paddlers
1710 Yahara Place
Madison, WI 53703
www.members.aol.com/Martinaxe/
madcity.html

Minnesota Canoe Association
P.O. Box 13567
Dinkytown Station
Minneapolis, MN 55414
www.canoe-kayak.org/

Negwegon Kayak Club
218 West Bay Street
East Tawas, MI 48703

North of Superior Canoe and Kayak Club
c/o Doug Bruce
POB 1696
Marathon, ON POT 2EO Canada

Peninsula Paddlers
822 North Fourth Avenue
Sturgeon Bay, WI 54235
www.geocities.com/Yosemite/Gorge/
9037/

Peninsula Paddlers (Niagara Peninsula)
Contacts:
In Niagara Falls, Eric at 905–354–1243
In Welland, Mary Jo at 905–735–9949
In Dundas, Louise at 905–628–3182

RASKAL
4805 South Lakeshore Drive
Racine, WI 53403–4127
www.execpc.com/~raskal

Sugar Island Canoe & Kayak Club
c/o Robert Jahn, Jr.
14 Deer Meadow Road
Warwick, NY 11222

Thunder Bay Kayak and Canoe Club
c/o Vicki Nikkola
210 Skyline Avenue
Thunder Bay, ON P7B 6K7 Canada

Twin Cities Sea Kayak Association
P.O. Box 581792
Minneapolis, MN 55458–1792
www.virtualmn.com/tcska/

University of Minnesota Kayak Club
108 Kirby Student Center, UMD
10 University Drive

Duluth, MN 55812–2496

Upper Midwest Kayak Touring News
P.O. Box 17115
Minneapolis, MN 55417–0115

West Michigan Coastal Kayakers Association
c/o Karl Giesel
1025 Griswold Southeast
Grand Rapids, MI 49507
www.iserv.net/~wmcka

Appendix B: Lessons, Rentals & Tours

Bay Creek Paddling Center
1099 Empire Boulevard
Rochester, NY 14609
(716) 288–2830
This shop offers rentals, lessons, and guided trips in the Rochester area.

Canyon Mountain
336 Princess Street
Kingston, Ontario
K7L 1B6 Canada
(613) 546–2276
(rentals only)

Caribou Expeditions
RR 2
76 Island Road
Goulais River, Ontario
POS 1EO, Canada
(800) 970–6662
www.sympatico.ca/caribouexp/
Offers sea kayak tours of Lake Superior and Lake Huron, and whale watching on the Saguenay fjord and the Gulf of St. Lawrence.

Expeditions et Decouvertes
Guide Aventure
250 Racine est c.p. 366
Chicoutimi (Québec)

G7H 5C2 Canada
(888) 545–4803
Provides guided trip of the Saguenay fjord and the Gulf of St. Lawrence, equipment, and many of their guides are bilingual.

G & S Watersports
Little Tub Harbour
Box 21
Tobermory, Ontario
N0H 2R0 Canada
(519) 596–2200
(rentals only)

The Great Outdoors/Les Cheneaux Kayak Adventures
44 M 134
P.O. Box 546
Cedarville, MI 49719
(906) 484–2011

Great River Outfitters
4180 Elizabeth Lake Road
Waterford, MI 48328
(248) 683–4770
Offers guided trips, rentals, lessons, and retail sales.

Huron Kayak J & P
Box 78

Paisley, Ontario
N0G 2N0 Canada
(519) 353–5572

Killarney Outfitters
Highway 637
Killarney, Ontario
POM 2AO Canada
(800) 461–1117

Mountain Equipment Coop
400 King Street West
Toronto, Ontario
M5V 1K2 Canada
(416) 340–2667
(rentals and classes only)

Pelee Wings
636 Point Pelee Drive
Leamington, Ontario
N8H 3V4 Canada
(519) 326–5193
(rentals only)

TI Adventures
38714 NYS 12E
Clayton, NY 13624
(315) 686–2000
(rentals only)

Tieken Kayaks
145 River Street
Gananoque (April–September)
(613) 382–2531
Mailing address:

Highway 7
Box 110
Chezzetcock, Nova Scotia
B0J 1N0 Canada
(rentals only)

Tobermory Adventure Tours
Box 241
Tobermory, Ontario
N0H 2R0 Canada
(519) 596–2289
(no rentals)

Trailhead
61 Front Street East
Toronto, Ontario
M5F 1B3 Canada
(416) 862–0881
(rentals and classes only)

White Squall
RR 1
Carling Bay Road
Nobel, Ontario
POG 1GO Canada
(705) 342–1975

White Squall Paddling Centre
RR1
Nobel, Ontario
P0G 1G0 Canada
(705) 746–4936
(rentals and guided tours only)

Appendix C: General Information

White Squall Paddling Center (RR 1, Carling Bay Road, Nobel, Ontario, POG 1GO Canada; 705–342–1975) puts on the Georgian Bay Kayak Symposium in mid-May, just in time to help you get ready for the paddling season. Call for information.

Stan and Emma Chladek were pioneers in introducing sea kayaking to the Great Lakes. For information on the Great Lakes Sea Kayak Symposium or other events, call Great River Outfitters at (248) 683–4770.

Index

Index

Acknowledgments

We are grateful to the many people who helped us in researching this book. In particular, we would like to thank Jan Brabant, David Brewster, Jack Elliot, Mike Geise, Al Kasinskas, Andy Kneply, Steve Lutsch, Michael Malone, Gary Nelkie, Mike Petzold, Sandy Richardson, Kathi Talley, Harry Tieken, Warren Williams, and the folks at Bay Creek Paddling Center (Rochester, New York) and The Great Outdoors (Cedarville, Michigan).